Don Green

Adrian Rogers

Mastering Your Emotions

ADRIAN P. ROGERS

MASTERING YOUR EMOTIONS

BROADMAN PRESS
Nashville, Tennessee

4250-65
ISBN: 0-8054-5065-3

Dewey Decimal Classification: 152.4
Subject Heading: EMOTIONS
Library of Congress Catalog Card Number: 88-6519
Printed in the United States of America

Library of Congress Cataloging-in-Publication Data

Rogers, Adrian.
Mastering your emotions / Adrian P. Rogers.
p. cm.
ISBN 0-8054-5065-3 : $9.95
1. Christian life—Baptist authors. 2. Emotions—Religious aspects—Christianity. I. Title.
BV4501.2.R6295 1988
248.4'86132—dc 19 88-6519
CIP

Dedication

This book is dedicated to Arden and Rose Rogers, my wonderful parents, and two of the most emotionally stable people I know. They have put into practice most of what is contained herein without the aid of technical study or conscious effort . . .

To Mom, whose wit and charm make her a joy to be around,

To Dad, whose positive attitude and warm friendship keep him perpetually young.

Introduction

Ogden Nash has said, "There is only one way to achieve happiness on this terrestrial ball, and that is to have either a clear conscience or none at all."

While I would not agree with that premise, I would say that a guilty conscience and other negative emotions can surely turn out the lights on your happiness.

And not only can negative emotions take life from your years, they can take years from your life.

In a recent university study it was shown that continuing hostile feelings can lead to illness and early death. When researchers followed up on personality studies of 118 law students done in the 1950s, they found that the most hostile in the group were more likely to die prematurely—from heart disease, cancer, thrombosis, and congestive heart failure—than those who showed few signs of hostility.

Indeed, we need to remember: when you are right, you can afford to keep your temper, and when you are wrong, you can't afford to lose it!

Today's emotional pressures are gigantic. Coping with hostilities, competition, financial stress, family demands, traffic jams, health problems, violence and crime puts staggering demands on fragile emotions.

There is no way we can make this emotional pressure evaporate, and one thing is for certain—either you will master your emotions or your emotions will master you.

This volume is to help you master such runaway emotions as: insecurity, depression, stress, frustration, inferiority, doubt, bewilderment, and bitterness.

I've heard of a little boy who was given the opportunity to choose a puppy for himself from a litter of puppies. His excited eyes fell on one wagging his tail. "I want the one with a happy ending," he said.

And a happy ending is what I want for you. Read on.

Contents

Mastering Your Emotions

1. All I Need—and More

He that doth the ravens feed
Yea, providentially caters for the sparrow,
Be comfort to my age! —Shakespeare

During recent years psychology and religion have had a field day with self-image—imaging, positive thinking, possibility thinking, self-realization, fulfillment, and the like. In the process all kinds of bizarre ideas have received ventilation.

What you think of yourself is exceedingly important. You can think too little or too much. A person can denigrate himself or deify himself. What is the proper slant? How should one feel about himself?

I can remember when it was thought pious to run oneself down. "I'm no good. I'm just a dirty dog. I deserve hell. I'm the pits." Many of the old hymns reflected this negative thinking. The problem is those Christians were focusing on the old life without Christ.

"All we like sheep have gone astray; we have turned every one to his own way, and the Lord hath laid on him the iniquity of us all" (Isa. 53:6). "There is none righteous, no, not one" (Rom. 3:10). "But we are all as an unclean thing, and all our righteousnesses are as filthy rags; and we all do fade away as a leaf; and our iniquities, like the wind, have taken us away" (Isa. 64:6). But these applied to us before we found our new life in Christ.

Ephesians 1 is an inspiration to the believer who is seeking a positive self-image.

> Paul, an apostle of Jesus Christ by the will of God, to the saints which are at Ephesus, and to the faithful in Christ Jesus: Grace be to you, and peace from God our Father, and from the Lord Jesus Christ. Blessed be the God and Father of our Lord Jesus Christ, who hath blessed us with all spiritual blessings in heavenly places in Christ: According as he hath chosen us in him before the foundation of the world, that we should be holy and without blame before him in love: Having predestinated us unto the adoption of children by Jesus Christ unto himself, according to the good pleasure of his will, To the praise of the glory of his grace, wherein he hath made us accepted in the beloved (1:1-6).

The Key to Everything.

A key phrase in this passage is "in Christ" or its equivalent. "In" is a small preposition, but a small key can open a vary large door.

The reason so many believers have a poor self-image is that they have never found out who they are *in Christ*. They remind me of the man who had an identity crisis and an energy crisis at the same time. He didn't know who he was, and he was too tired to find out!

But I want you to understand this: Christianity is not behavior modification. You see, God does not work from the outside in. God does not modify our behavior in order to change us. God changes us *from within* in order to modify our behavior. Sin is an inside job, and when God deals with sin, He works *on the inside first*. God changes the heart.

In Ephesians, Paul first tells us who we are in Christ. (chapter 1); then he tells us how we came to be who we are in Christ (chapters 2 and 3); and finally he tells us how to live like who we are in Christ. (chapters 4 through 6). Paul treats the *being* aspect before he goes into the *doing*.

If you personally turn that order around, you will fall into the deadly trap of legalism. It is frustrating to live contrary to an identity you do not have in your heart and mind.

Jesus declared, "Ye shall know the truth, and the truth shall make you free" (John 8:32). The truth frees us, and what is the truth? The truth is what God says. And that truth is embodied in the Lord Jesus.

But the truth does not make you free until you know it. You must embrace the doctrinal before you can turn it into the practical. God's truth is absolute, and it is absolutely true.

Once a marine biologist observed a northern pike in an aquarium. For a while the biologist turned loose all the minnows that pike could eat, and he gorged himself. Then a trick was pulled. A glass cylinder was dropped into the tank, and the minnows were put into the cylinder. The pike kept trying to reach the minnows in the cylinder and finally gave up.

Then the biologist released all those minnows. They swam right past the pike's mouth, and he never made a move for them. The fish starved with all of that food around him. He became a slave to false perception, as many of us Christians do. The pike's false perception based on previous facts killed him.

Mr. Average Christian does not understand who he is in Christ. He has a first-class ticket, but he is riding in the fourth-class car. He does not comprehend the riches that reside within him. He is free in Christ but not liberated in the truest sense. He is thinking in the past tense when he was bound by the old life. He protests, "I cannot succeed. I cannot be free. I am chained by a habit. I am bogged down. I am a failure, and I am hampered by my limited knowledge." If he believes such, it might as well be true, for all practical purposes.

Plastic surgeons report that many people are still dissatisfied with themselves after nose jobs, tummy tucks, facelifts, and cosmetic surgery all over their bodies. Doctors reveal that many radiantly beautiful women bodily and facially cannot stand themselves. That is often true with handsome men. The anorexic girl thinks of herself as fat, even though she is emaciated and starving to death. Self-perception!

Christian, perhaps you have misread yourself. You are letting life at its fullest swim on by. You are emotionally and spiritually hungry, but you will not eat the hidden manna God has for you.

There are three qualities you want, whether or not you admit the fact: 1. You want *significance*. 2. You want *sufficiency*. 3. You want *security*. You need those even as you need food and water.

But I want to dwell on three positive statements which will enable you to have a self-image God intends for you. First of all,

RECOGNIZE YOUR RIGHTEOUSNESS

Paul wrote to "the saints which are in Ephesus" (v. 1). There are only two kinds of folks, the saints and "the ain'ts." You are either fully saved or not saved at all. There are no special categories of Christians. Every blood-bought, born-again believer is a saint, whether or not he feels like it. Saint means a set-apart, sanctified person, one God has made righteous and has set apart.

We ought to affirm it. "I am Saint Adrian." "I am Saint Joe." "I am Saint Joyce." "I am Saint Mary." And we have every right to call ourselves "saint." People have remarked, "How arrogant." No, it is not. We have the righteousness of God within our lives.

More Christians have a mock humility, and it can be disgusting. They ought to quit alibiing. We confuse stooped posture for humility. No wonder we have trouble convincing people they ought to become Christians. True humility is through Christ. Mock humility is laid upon us by none other than the devil.

It is tragic, but many will never accept their sainthood. A while back there was a fad for believers to make comments like, "I'm saved, but I'm not a Christian." Then the person would explain, "Well, I'm not worthy to call myself a Christian because I'm not living like one." That is preposterous.

Let me nail it down. You are the next of kin to the Trinity. You are a prince or a princess. Why? Because you are a child of the King. Since you are a part of God's family, Jesus is not only your Lord and Savior, but He is your Friend and Brother. "You have no other such a Friend or Brother, Tell it to Jesus alone."

True humility is not thinking negatively about yourself. It is agreeing with what God says about you. The grace of God will exalt a person without inflating him and will humble a person without debasing him. When you see who you really are, you begin to confess it.

I am what I am—a saint. Therefore, I have significance. I am a VIP in Christ. I am going to reign and rule with Him, and I am reigning with Him now.

No, in this life you are not going to be sinless, but as you deal with sin in your life, you can come closer and closer to being free from sin. *Sinless no but blameless yes*. As you confess and stay prayed up, you can be blameless.

> According as he hath chosen us in him before the foundation of the world, that we should be holy and without blame before him in love (v. 4).

"Holy and without blame before him in love." When God the Father sees the blood of His Son upon you, He sees you as perfect. In Ephesians, Paul writes about the grace of God. In Romans 4:4 he says, "Now to him that worketh is the reward not reckoned of grace, but of debt." If we could earn our salvation, God would be in debt to us, but the reverse is true. "But to him that worketh not, but believeth on him that justifieth the ungodly, his faith is counted for righteousness" (Rom. 4:5).

Verse 6 refers to David describing the blessedness of the man to whom righteousness is imputed. Imputed means to put that on your account. So, what has God done? He has put the righteousness of the Lord Jesus on your account. Today we use the word *charge*. We have various purchases put on our account.

How am I righteous? How are you? And why are we? Because the Lord Jesus has laid His righteousness on us. Romans 4:6-8 makes it crystal clear:

> Even as David also describeth the blessedness of the man, unto whom God imputeth righteousness without works, Saying, Blessed are they whose iniquities are forgiven, whose sins are covered. Blessed is the man to whom the Lord will not impute sin.

Notice the contrasts of the word impute. In Christ we will have the righteousness of Christ imputed to us. Those outside of Christ will have the ledger of sin imputed to their account. I care not the temptations and trials you face as a Christian, you are righteous in God's sight.

Now follows one of the most amazing truths concerning our righteousness and how it was secured: "He made Him who knew no sin to be sin on our behalf, that we might become the righteousness of God in Him" (1 Cor. 5:21, NASB). Jesus was made the embodiment of sin itself on our behalf in order that we would become righteous in Him.

You will not behave as you should until you have the biblical concept of who you are and how you ought to respond. It is a proven fact: children—and adults—who have a poor self-concept set out to live their shabby feelings. Our jails and prisons are crammed with people who have bad feelings about themselves.

So many speak of themselves as "a sinner saved by grace." In the technical sense that may be true, but the Bible definition of a saint is "the righteousness of God in Christ." But someone argues, "If you don't keep reminding someone of his sinfulness he will be careless concerning ain." Oh? Let me ask you this question—Who is more afraid of dirt—a man in grimy overalls or one in a white tuxedo?

We are so experienced in confessing our sins, but when are we going to learn to confess our righteousness? It is ours, bought and paid for by the shed blood of Christ.

How could we possibly be ashamed of such a costly gift? Yet, the Spirit will help us keep our feelings in balance. D. L. Moody commented, "The more one talks about his own holiness and righteousness, the less holy and righteous he is." When we confess our righteousness, we must make it known: it is His righteousness given to us as a gift of grace. "For I say, through the grace given unto me, to every man that is among you, not to think of himself more highly than he ought to think; but to think soberly, according as God hath dealt to every man the measure of faith" (Rom. 12:3).

If you would have a healthy, positive self-image, you must recognize your righteousness, and your righteousness does not relate to your works at all. "In my hand no price I bring, Simply to Thy Cross I cling."

From the Word of God I would suggest that you . . .

RELY ON YOUR RESOURCES

How many of my readers have all the love, patience, courage, wisdom, and faith they need? "Not me," you answer. Ah, but if you are saved, you do! "Blessed be the God and Father of our Lord Jesus Christ, who hath blessed us with all spiritual blessings in heavenly places in Christ." He has already blessed us. As R. A. Torrey phrased it, "We have inexhaustible supplies for every need." There is a reservoir, a storehouse of blessing which God has for us. God has already blessed us with all spiritual blessings, all things that pertain to life and godliness—not some but *all*.

As a believer in Christ Jesus you have everything you need. You do. *Everything*. All of it. Nothing is lacking with God. You don't understand? Let me illustrate.

After the death of Moses, God commissioned Joshua and gave him a promise: "Every place that the sole of your foot shall tread upon, that have I given unto you, as I said unto Moses" (Josh. 1:3). Joshua and the Israelites had to tread the land to possess it. God had given it, but they had to possess their possessions. They had to put the foot of faith on the provisions of God. Most of us have shelves of unread books. Even though we call them *our* books, they are not really ours until we read them. It is not enough to talk about the resources of Christ if we never call upon them. God Almighty has all you need, but you must claim it.

It is not necessary to long for more love, more patience, more understanding, more this or that in the Christian life. God has it for you. All you have to do is call upon those resources.

Several years ago Peter Lord was preaching for us. Peter has profound insight from the Lord. What a grand name—Lord! Before the service he asked one of our deacons, Gene Howard, if he could slip a ten-dollar bill into his wife, Betty's, Bible without her knowledge. Gene agreed to do it.

Then, in the middle of the service, Peter looked at Betty and called on her to come up front as a "volunteer." Gene made sure Betty had her Bible with her.

Peter asked, "Betty, do you believe I am a man of God? Do you believe I would lie to you? Do you trust me? Do you love me in Jesus?" To all those questions she answered "yes."

"OK," Peter continued, "if you believe in me and love me, then if I asked you to do something reasonable for me, would you do it? It is something you can do right here where you are." "Sure" came the reply.

"All right, then, would you please give me ten dollars?" Betty blushed and answered, "But I don't have ten dollars." So, Peter then asked, "Is that your Bible?"

"Yes, it is," she replied. "Hand it here, please," Peter requested. He looked in it and lifted out that ten-dollar bill. He inquired, "Why didn't you give it to me?"

To which she said, "But I didn't know it was there. How did it get in there?"

Peter explained his whole point, "I put it in there. All I was asking you to do was give me what I had already given to you."

Now underline this three times in red. Our good and gracious God is never going to ask us for anything He has not already given us! "All things." "All things are Thine, No gift have we, Lord of all gifts to offer Thee." All things are His, and then He gives them to us.

Before the late and great Dr. R. G. Lee died I was in his home with Billy Graham, Cliff Barrows, and Tommy Lane, our minister of music at Bellevue Church. Dr. Lee was one of my predecessors at Bellevue, considered perhaps the best preacher of the twentieth century and one of the greatest in the history of Christianity. His adopted daughter came out and gravely announced, "I believe Dr. Lee is dying." We were shocked. An elderly doctor rushed over and found that Dr. Lee was alive but unconscious.

Because we thought he was close to being with Jesus, Tommy suggested, "Let's sing him into heaven." So we sang as best we could "Majestic Sweetness Sits Enthroned," Dr. Lee's favorite hymn. Then Cliff Barrows led us in "Come Thou Angel Band." I was ready to enter heaven myself.

Then Dr. Lee revived and opened his piercing blue eyes, and his daughter said, "Papa, Billy Graham is here." Dr. Lee pulled Billy's head down and kissed him. Later, Dr. Lee testified, "I saw heaven. I saw Jesus. I saw my mother. I never did justice to heaven in my sermons." You say he was hallucinating? Oh, how I hope God gives me an hallucination like that!

I asked, "Dr. Lee, when God calls you on, is there some way we could put your brain in my head?" He replied, with a twinkle in his eyes, "That would be like putting a grand piano in a closet!"

Even better than having Dr. Lee's brain is to have the Son of God in me. And He is. He dwells in our lives. What more can we ask?

Through the years I have heard some talk about "the second blessing." By the second blessing they have meant an encounter with the Holy Spirit after the initial salvation experience. They have called it "baptism in the Spirit" or "baptism by the Spirit."

I am not being disrespectful, but I believe the second blessing is understanding what you got in the first one! I believe many Christians draw closer to the Lord and begin to understand what the first blessing means, and that is so radical they think of it as an entirely different encounter with the Lord, when actually it may be an affirmation of their identity in Jesus.

While we are on this: if you ever were saved, the Holy Spirit is already in you. He has you. You have Him. If you are born again into God's family, you don't have to "get the Holy Ghost." He is with you. "Now if any man have not the Spirit of Christ, he is none of his" (Rom. 8:9*b*). If you do not have the Holy Spirit, you are not saved.

So, the second blessing, I feel, is finally understanding what the first blessing, being born again, means to you.

When you are saved, you receive it all. *All* blessings. God does not give His Spirit by measure. All the spiritual blessings are yours. Have you relied on the resources?

You ever hear of the *third blessing?* No. The third blessing is discovering you didn't discover it all the second time. And the fourth one is still discovering there is more. You will spend the rest of your life being amazed by the resources which are available. "God has blessed us with all spiritual blessings in heavenly places in Christ Jesus." The next time you need love, don't pray, "Lord help me to use my love." Rather, by faith pray, "Lord Jesus, you live in me—not my love but Thy love. I cannot love, but You can." You will be amazed at the result.

Realize your righteousness. Recognize it. Rely upon your resources in Christ. Third of all,

REST IN YOUR RELATIONSHIP

> To the praise of the glory of his grace, wherein he hath made us accepted in the beloved (Eph. 1:6).

How desperately we want acceptance and security! Only demented persons long for rejection. Americans beat their brains out to be accepted. We buy things we don't need with money we don't have to impress people we don't even like. We try to keep up with the Joneses, but when we finally catch up with them, they refinance.

We hear about peer pressure all the time. When I was a kid we had none of those fancy terms, but we wanted to be liked. We recognized that there was a standard in school and at play. If you were different in actions, attitudes, clothes, and the like, you were "out" and not popular. And children, bless them, can be cruel.

Madison Avenue has made multiplied millions by playing on people's innate desires to have acceptance. We are conditioned to believe that to be accepted means to drive a certain car or dress according to Vidal or Yves or Pierre.

In Christ you are already accepted in the beloved. Here is a remarkable fact—He loves you perfectly (1 John 4:18). This gives security. It is not our perfect love for Him but His perfect love for us that makes the difference. *There is nothing you can do to make Him love you more*. His perfect love casts out fear. *There is also nothing that will cause Him to love us less*.

You are accepted right now. God does not change you so He can love you—He loves you so He can change you. This may sound revolutionary, but God loves you as much as He love Jesus. "I in them, and thou in me, that they may be made perfect in one; and that the world may know that thou hast sent me, and hast loved them, as thou hast loved me" (John 17:23) "As thou hast loved me." That's how God loves you! "Behold, what manner of love the Father hath bestowed upon us, that we should be called the sons of God" (1 John 3:1*a*). Jesus is not ashamed to call us His brothers and sisters. That is security and acceptance.

Throughout the New Testament there occurs and recurs that meaningful phrase, "in Christ." Think of the security bound up in those two words—"in Christ." Let me illustrate. Noah's ark is a picture of Christ, according to the apostle Peter. God had invited Noah, "Come into the ark." That means God was already in the ark. Once Noah came in, God shut the door. God not only shut the water out, God shut Noah in. Noah was in the ark like we are in Christ. Noah was as safe as the ark was safe, and we are as safe as Christ is safe.

Some believe we have security only after we arrive in heaven. But wait a minute! The angels fell from heaven. If you are not secure here, you would not be secure there. Security is not in a place but in a Person—Jesus. Noah may have fallen down in the ark, but he never fell out of it!

We have this security. We also have significance and sufficiency. "Who could ask for anything more?"

God has accomplished all of this "to the praise of the glory of His grace."

- God has accepted me through the death and resurrection of Jesus, His Son. *That is grace.*
- By faith I accept the fact that He accepts me. *That is faith. Faith is my acceptance of God's acceptance of me.*
- I then am able to accept myself. *That is peace.*
- Because of all the foregoing, I am then free to accept you. *That is love.* I am free to give, and I can relate to you in love because there is plenty where that came from.
- Finally you can accept me. I am no longer grasping at you, trying to manipulate you, trying to use you. *Your acceptance of me is koinonia—fellowship.*

That chain of acceptance was initiated by the amazing grace of God!

You are in Christ. And where is He? Seated in the heavenlies. You are also seated in those heavenly places, even though you still have your address on planet Earth. You are enthroned with Him. You "are more than conquerors through him that loved us" (Rom. 8:37).

Barbara Taylor writes about this passage of Scripture in Ephesians 1:

> REASONS I HAVE TODAY TO BLESS GOD, THE FATHER OF OUR LORD JESUS CHRIST: HE HAS BLESSED US WITH EVERY SPIRITUAL BLESSING. THESE BLESSINGS ARE LOCATED IN THE HEAVENLY PLACES IN CHRIST. GOD HAS CHOSEN US IN CHRIST BEFORE THE FOUNDATION OF THE WORLD. HIS CHOICE WAS THAT WE SHOULD BE HOLY AND WITHOUT BLAME BEFORE HIM IN LOVE. HE HAS PREDESTINATED US AS SONS BY JESUS CHRIST TO HIMSELF. THIS ALL WAS TO THE GOOD PLEASURE OF HIS WILL AND TO THE PRAISE OF

THE GLORY OF HIS GRACE. IT WAS BY THIS GRACE THAT HE HAS MADE US . . .

ACCEPTED IN THE BELOVED![1]

The never-failing security the believer has in Christ dispels the ahakiness of insecurity. Priscilla J. Owens summed it up well in her song "We Have an Anchor":

We have an anchor that keeps the soul
Steadfast and sure while the billows roll,
Fastened to the Rock which cannot move,
Grounded firm and deep in the Saviour's love.

NOTE

1. Barbara Taylor, *From Rejection to Acceptance* (Nashville: Broadman Press, 1987), pp. 187-188.

Depression

2. A Cure for the Blues

Be still, sad heart! and cease repining;
Behind the clouds is the sun still shining.

—Longfellow

Dr. John Stott once remarked that the Christian's chief occupational hazards are depression and discouragement. And how!

Have you ever been depressed? Have you ever been helpless or hopeless, sort of feeling there was not much to live for? Have you suffered through a case of the blues? Maybe you were not even sure why depression had strangled your joy and zest for living.

Most all of us have a general notion of what depression entails. Depression is characterized by emotions of helplessness or hopelessness which lead to sadness. A person who is depressed has problems real or imagined, and he does not seem to have a grasp on a solution. He may think there is nothing to snap him out of his doldrums. A feeling of helplessness and hopelessness leads to a deep despondency.

Most of us would concur, "Yes, I have been depressed. Sometimes I am depressed for long periods of time, sometimes only a few hours." And others would be honest enough to confess, "I am depressed right now. I just want to fade away or even die."

Many people who have studied the Bible have commented to me, "I want to be like those heroes and heroines of the Bible. They weren't like me, all upset and emotional, going up and down, and depressed."

Really? The fact is: the Bible paints a candid picture of its greatest men and women and all they suffered as flesh-and-blood human beings. They contended with and grappled with all kinds of emotions, healthy and unhealthy. They were not demigods.

Moses was the supreme Lawgiver of God. The Lord spoke to him and called him to deliver the people of Israel. Surely he had mastery over his emotions. Right? Wrong!

Read his prayer in Numbers 11:15. You may be astonished as you review his plea. Moses remonstrated with the Lord and prayed:

> And if thou deal thus with me, kill me, I pray thee, out of hand, if I have found favour in thy sight; and let me not see my wretchedness.

He begged God to take him home. As many have done through the centuries, he asked the Lord to remove him from the land of the living, "You do it, Lord. Kill me."

Lay all of the miserable adjectives on Moses—suicidal, depressed, discouraged, wretched, you name it. He was so abysmally low he wanted to die. At least he claimed that he desired death. He was linking the love and favor of God, God's grace, with his death wish. Astounding, but it is right there in the Bible.

First Kings 19:4 is going to sound familiar. Elijah, on the heels of a resounding victory over the prophets of Baal on Mount Carmel, fell into the pit of depression. He hied himself a day's journey into the wilderness from Beersheba and . . .

> came and sat down under a juniper tree; and he requested for himself that he might die; and said, It is enough; now, O Lord, take away my life; for I am not better than my fathers.

He had "had it." Elijah felt he was worse off than "between a rock and a hard place." He had arrived, he thought, at "wit's end corner."

In fright he sought a solution through flight, flight first to Beersheba and then into the desolate wilderness, and then flight by wanting to fly away to the Lord through death. If only we would admit it, many of us have done the same. Many have explained to me, "Preacher, I came to the place in my life and experience where I wanted to die. In fact, I prayed to die."

Then consider the case of Jonah, the petulant prophet. In Jonah 4:3 there is another one of these bewildering prayers:

> Therefore now, O Lord, take, I beseech thee, my life from me; for it is better for me to die than to live.

How similar are these petitions! Kill me. "Stop the world, I want to get off."

Can you imagine these men of God praying like that? Many adults have never recognized the import of these prayers because they have given only a cursory, fleeting approach to the Bible. Yes, the Word of God is filled with the foibles and frustrations of the men and women of God.

Moses and Elijah were representative of the Law and the Prophets. God Himself chose them from all of the Old Testament saints to appear with Jesus in His Mount of Transfiguration experience.

> And after six days Jesus taketh Peter, James, and John his brother, and bringeth them up into an high mountain apart, And was transfigured before them: and his face did shine as the sun, and his raiment was white as the light. And, behold, there appeared unto them Moses and Elias [Elijah] talking with him (Matt. 17:1-3).

Surely men of that caliber would "have it all together" and be impervious to the onslaught of depression—but no. Jonah was signally set apart in that his being three days and three nights in the belly of the great fish was compared by Jesus to His own entombment and resurrection (see Jon. 1:17*ff*.; Matt. 12:40).

But we must remember these men were frail human beings, men "of like passions." They were subject to feelings and emotions. *There were reasons for their depression*. Sometimes there seems to be none for ours, but there are root causes just the same.

Before we examine in detail their problems (why they were depressed) and the provisions from God (how they were able to overcome their depression), let me enumerate the phases of depression:

A passive or listless feeling.
Sadness.
An attitude of "nothing seems to matter."
A feeling of helplessness.
A feeling of hopelessness.
An attitude of feeling nothing is ever going to get better.
An idea that no one cares or understands.
A sense of rejection.
An emotion of "I would be better off dead."
A desire for death.

Face it. Nearly all of us have experienced at least a few of those emotions, if not all of them, to one degree or another.

Let's look at . . .

THEIR PROBLEMS

Before we can deal with our depression and accept the provisions for our cure, it is helpful to examine the root causes. Nearly all psychologists and psychiatrists agree that depression is caused by physical, emotional, or mental factors, or either a combination of them all.

Nelson Price has classified four types of depression:

endogenous: caused by a chemical imbalance within the central nervous system; often associated with some observable external cause

reactive: a reaction to such things as the death of a loved one, a severe personal setback (divorce from a spouse, breakup with a sweetheart, loss of a job, and the like)

toxic: caused by outside substances such as viral illness, drugs, or a faulty diet *psychotic:* linked to "nervous breakdown," over-exhaustion, mental disorder, or brain disease

According to therapists, the first two, endogenous and reactive, seem to account for the majority of cases of depression.[1]

We can discover the problems of Moses, Elijah, and Jonah from the context of their prayers. Each of them seems to face three major problems: physical, psychological, and spiritual problems.

Physical Depletion.

Moses, Elijah, and Jonah, first of all, were *physically drained,* worn out, "worn to a frazzle." It is logical to begin with Moses. What could have precipitated his strange prayer for God to kill him?

Numbers 11 opens with the people of Israel complaining. They were chronic bellyachers. They remind you of little Goldilocks. "This bed's too hard. This bed's too soft. This bed's just right." The only difference is: to many of the Israelites all of the beds would have been unacceptable! They groused about the weather, the food, the provisions, the leadership of Moses, and every conceivable aspect of their lives. "The people cried unto Moses" (v. 2). And cried and cried and cried.

Moses was leading an estimated two million people through the desert from Egypt toward Canaan, the Promised Land, where he would never set foot. In spite of the bondage in Egypt, many of them longed for a return to slavery, if only they could eat the onions, spices, and herbs of Egypt. They pined for the fleshpots of Egypt, including the meat. They had forsaken God's especially prepared manna, no doubt the most nutritious food ever concocted.

"Who shall give us flesh to eat?" they griped. They remembered the fish in Egypt, the cucumbers, melons, leeks, and garlic. "But now our soul is dried away: there is nothing at all, beside this manna, before our eyes" (vv. 4-6).

Here is the key to his depression.

> I am not able to bear all this people alone, because it is too heavy for me (v. 14).

He was physically depleted from the administrative responsibility of guiding the people. He had unbelievable burdens pressing on him.

Workaholics and non-workaholics can learn from the depression of Moses. Many a businessman works late at night and sometimes over the weekend, fearful of losing his position and weighted down with stressful tasks. The housewife who has several children, and sometimes very little appreciation from her husband and children, often breaks down, but "a woman's work is never done," so she has to continue her household duties. The children are crying and fussy. There is a house to clean, beds to make, the shopping to do, the garbage to empty, and a thousand and one chores often not shared by her husband and children.

The conscientious pastor is often in the same predicament as Moses. Instead of a shared ministry, many pastors have to carry the load virtually by themselves. They are literally called on around the clock. Too many of them fail even to take a vacation. "Mary had a little lamb. It grew to be a sheep. It then became a pastor and died from lack of sleep." How true.

Moses was at that juncture. He cried to God, "I can't bear it. I can't stand it."

Likewise, Elijah had been fasting for a long time. Even though Jehovah was standing with him, the pressure and strain were murderous. He was emotionally strung out, and he had finished a run of Marathon proportions. His strength was gone. He was hungry, thirsty, and totally exhausted. His symptoms were almost the same as those of Moses. The physical exertion had taken its toll (1 Kings 19:3-4*ff.*).

And think of Jonah who had a whale house for a jail house. He spent those three nights on a "foam blubber mattress." And he had preached a city-wide crusade in a city the size of Memphis, Tennessee, including women and children.

He had no posh motel or hotel room. No one offered him room and board. If they did it is not mentioned in the Word. He had no mule or donkey. There were no advance man and no follow-up staff either. There was no public address system, and he preached as he walked from one end of that sinful metropolis to the other.

The sirocco, that blast-furnace-hot wind from the desert, blew upon his tortured body. The unbearable desert sun blazed down on him. He almost underwent a sunstroke. Twice in chapter 4 Jonah expresses the wish to die.

> Therefore now, O Lord, take, I beseech thee, my life from me; for it is better for me to die than to live (v. 3). And it came to pass, when the sun did arise, that God prepared a vehement east wind; and the sun beat upon the head of Jonah, that he fainted, and wished in himself to die, and said, It is better for me to die than to live (v. 8).

When you are physically worn out—your nutrition is bad, your sleep fitful or scarce, your nerves frayed with pressure and anxiety—you are a prime candidate for an attack of depression.

In addition to physical problems, they were also beset with *psychological problems*. From time to time all of us have difficulties with our emotions. A song went, "Feelings, nothing more than feelings . . ." but feelings are potent and color every facet of our lives. Those who boast, "Why, I don't ever have problems with my emotions or feelings," may sometimes have the most knotty impediments of all.

Psychological Duress.

Moses had a *psychological problem with people* which profoundly affected his slant on life. He had his eyes on other people. He moaned to the Lord, "Wherefore hast thou afflicted thy servant? and wherefore have I not found favour in thy sight, that thou layest the burden of all this people upon me?" (Num. 11:11). "I am not able to bear all this burden alone, because it is too heavy for me" (Num. 11:14).

Many a pastor, for instance, falls into that psychological trap. Deep down inside he begins to recoil from people, the very people God has called him to lead and serve. He thinks, *I don't believe I can stand it much longer. Everytime my folks come to me, there's a problem. I love them—I really do—but inside I have trouble liking them.*

Moses pled with the Lord, "Lord, you have laid the burden of this people on me." He had learned you don't have to be a cannibal to get fed up with people!

Our own Lord and Savior faced the same situation. The Gospels speak about the "press" of the crowds around Him, the jostling, pushing, and shoving of the people vying for His attention. It was true with Moses as people continually badgered him. "Give us this. Solve that problem. Negotiate this dispute."

Moses' fuse was becoming short, and he was emotionally overloaded. And depression often sets in when we are emotionally taxed.

> And it came to pass on the morrow, that Moses sat to judge the people: and the people stood by Moses from the morning unto the evening (Ex. 18:13).

That one verse is fraught with meaning. "On the morrow" is noteworthy. Not only did Moses have to contend with tomorrow when it arrived, but he possibly fretted about tomorrow the night before! The businessman often dreads the events of tomorrow on the night before. That is true with most of us. There is not only the grim prospect of tasks we would like to avoid altogether but also the simmering and stewing over them even before the time comes.

Depression often sets in when we are overloaded and overworked. Exodus 18:14 is rather unusual:

> And when Moses' father in law saw all that he did to the people, he said, What is this thing that thou doest to the people? Why sittest thou thyself alone, and all the people stand by thee from morning unto even?

What did Jethro mean? The indication is: "Moses, you are not being fair to the people or to yourself. How can you do it by yourself?" "And Moses' father in law said unto him, The thing that thou doest is not good. Thou wilt surely wear away, both thou, and this people that is with thee: for this thing is too heavy for thee; thou art not able to perform it thyself alone (Ex. 18:17-18).

Isn't that plain, and wasn't Jethro wise? He was counseling Moses not to do it by himself. Moses' approach was breaking him and the people down. For one reason or another Moses was trying to be a martyr. "The martyr complex" is often associated with cases of depression. "Poor me, I alone care. Only I have all of the answers. No one else is able to counsel and make decisions."

This mistaken notion is the downfall of many a preacher. A preacher who is always available to accept every assignment, to pray at every civic club, to attend every community meeting, and to serve on every committee may not be much worth when he is available. Here was Moses from can to can't, from daybreak to sunset, counseling and judging and arguing and . . .

Businessman, your work will still be there Monday, unless a tornado sweeps it away, but as soon as possible the company will locate more piles of paperwork. That is also true of the housewife. You can never do it all. All work and no play will make Jack and Jill a dull boy and girl. Worse than that, it can make Jack and Jill depressed.

Here is a thought we might as well admit. Depression is often meshed with anger. Moses was angry. Elijah was angry. Jonah was angry.

Barbara Taylor, in her book *From Rejection to Acceptance,* writes about anger and depression:

> Many Christian leaders who talk about anger and depression believe they are tied together, whether or not the person victimized by them understands the logistics of them. Among these are Tim LaHaye and Charles Solomon. Solomon has expressed that depression is really at heart an "internal temper tantrum." . . . Tim LaHaye says in his book

How to Win Over Depression, "The first step in the chain reaction producing depression is anger. Don't be surprised that you involuntarily reject such a proposal. I have consistently observed that most depressed persons cannot and do not think of themselves as angry people."[2]

Moses had a *people problem*. But Elijah was burdened down with a *psychological problem* of self-pity. Elijah had every reason to be triumphant. God had answered his prayer with fire from heaven, and the forces of Baal were slain and scattered. He should have been "sitting on top of the world." Elijah had "The Post-revival Blues," and he began to drink from the intoxicating cup of self-pity.

Psychologically, Elijah has been called one of the most complex personages in the Bible. Perhaps a number of factors entered into his dark depression. Earlier we dealt with the anatomy of his depression from 1 Kings 19. He requested of the Lord that he might die and said, "It is enough; now, O Lord, take away my life; for I am not better than my fathers" (v. 4).

It is not easy to sum up Elijah's psychological workings. He was "a man of like passions." After his mountaintop experience at Carmel, he almost immediately "bottomed out" into the valley. Jezebel, to this day the epitome of wickedness, then threatened his life, making a vow to have him killed. And he virtually ran the length of Palestine trying to escape her. He was not the last preacher to become depressed over a long-tongued Jezebel or a weak-kneed Ahab who was hiding behind his wife's skirts.

So many people make suicidal threats, and yet do not really want to die—but they are enervated from psychological, physical, and spiritual problems. Elijah was wallowing in self-pity. If he had really wanted to die, all he would have needed to do was stand still. Jezebel would have done him in.

Jonah had a *pout problem*. He questioned what God was doing. God spared the Ninevites, but it infuriated Jonah. Jonah had foretold the destruction of that city, and when God spared the people, it hurt Jonah's pride and angered him, because then the people might think he was a false prophet.

Jonah felt the sinful Ninevites deserved destruction, and he did not want to deliver a message of deliverance. Nothing is more indicative of Jonah's poutiness than his exchange with the Lord in Jonah 4.

> But it displeased Jonah exceedingly, and he was very angry. And he prayed unto the Lord, and said, I pray thee, O Lord, was not this my saying, when I was yet in my country? Therefore I fled before unto Tarshish: for I know that thou art a gracious God, and merciful, slow to anger, and of great kindness, and repentest thee of the evil. Therefore now, O Lord, take, I beseech thee, my life from me; for it is better for me to die than to live. Then said the Lord, Doest thou well to be angry? (vv. 1-4).

He was a super patriot. He loved Israel, and his spiteful feelings toward Nineveh were akin to those many have toward Libya and Iran in these days. "Look what they have done to God's people," they say. You have seen those bumper stickers: "Bomb Iran," "Kill the Ayatollah," and the like.

Jonah was further depressed because of his conflict. He was the prophet of God, and he all too well understood the gracious, loving character of God. Somehow I believe Jonah wanted to rejoice in the deliverance of Nineveh because it was a testimony to his God. Yet he had trouble bringing himself to that point. His depression naturally sprang from his profound spiritual struggle and fear of national loss.

Depression often arises as a result of losing someone or something we deeply value—a husband or wife, a close friend, a sweetheart, a prized possession, a hope. You thought you were going to receive that promotion, but someone less qualified and with less seniority did.

Depression can also come as a result of a threatened or impending loss. A woman's husband walks in one night and announces, "I don't love you anymore. I am moving out." The wife falls into a deep depression over the threatened loss of her husband. In some cases they may still be together "until death doth part them." We can have an unresolved grief, and that can turn to bitterness and anger.

Before each one of these men asked God to take them, they had deep, emotional, psychological problems. Moses had his eyes upon others. Elijah had his eyes upon himself. Jonah had his eyes upon circumstances. None of them at the moment truly had their eyes upon God. They were emotionally wrung out.

Spiritual Disrepair.

Not only were they *physically worn out,* not only were they *emotionally wrung out,* but they became *spiritually run down*. Why were they run down?

The devil, our enemy, is a master strategist. He knows exactly when to move in on you and attack when you are in a fit of self-pity, self-centeredness, and despondency. When you remove your eyes from the Lord, you are especially vulnerable to Satan's attack.

Until God stepped in with the answer, and until they were willing to accept it, they were in a bad state of spiritual disrepair. I do not believe one can pray like this and not have a gaping spiritual need in his/her life. Now you thought no Christian could feel like that, didn't you? Surely a person can't pray like that and be saved. Right? Wrong! These were the cream of the crop for God, but they reached that low point.

Now, when did they fall into trouble spiritually? When they were already vulnerable. You are buffeted by Satan when you are weak emotionally, physically, and psychologically. In this kind of predicament you are a sitting duck for the negative emotions of the devil. God "hath not given us the spirit of fear; but of power, and of love, and of a sound mind" (2 Tim. 1:7). God authors these in the hearts and minds of those who are totally caught up in Him. But when we do not avail ourselves of God's provision, we are ripe for Satanic attack.

Depression often sets in when we are coming off of a tremendous emotional high. Each of these men had experienced incomparable spiritual victories.

Moses had seen the hand of God in His judgment of the Egyptians and in the Israelites' dry-shod passage through the Red Sea. Surely he would have remained on the mountain top. Yet, he was down in the valley, praying to die.

Elijah prayed to die after the tumultuous victory on Mount Carmel. The people had fallen on their faces and exclaimed, "The Lord, He is God!" God had stood with him in the showdown with 450 heathenish priests of Baal. Then he ran from one painted woman. On the heels of a heavenly miracle there was the depression of a letdown.

Jonah beheld the saving power of God, and an entire city repented in sackcloth and ashes. He plummeted into an emotional pit. Leonard Ravenhill has observed that when God opens the windows of heaven to bless us, the devil will open the windows of hell to blast us,

You and I have faced those periods of "post-revival blues." It is almost like the letdown many experience after Christmas—only far worse. It reminds you of the song which goes, "Flying high in April, shot down in May."

Nonetheless, we should not be afraid of high spiritual emotions. Our own Lord had undergone marvelous spiritual experiences. He was baptized as an example for us, the Spirit of God descended upon Him, and the Father spoke of His pleasure, "This is my beloved Son, in whom I am well pleased" (Matt. 3:17). Immediately (Matt. 4:1) He was "led up of the Spirit into the wilderness to be tempted of the devil." He was worn out physically as He fasted forty days and forty nights, being tempted and tried by the enemy.

Jesus is our example as He combated the devil with the Word of God. Three times he quoted verses from Deuteronomy. Jesus defeated the devil, and through Christ, you can too.

Jesus always kept His eyes on the Father, and He was reliant on the power of the Holy Spirit.

Moses, Elijah, and Jonah did not always look to God. They gazed at self, at others, at circumstances. Any Christian who does that is going to become depressed.

There was a physical reason, a psychological reason, and a spiritual reason for their depression. Physically worn out, emotionally wrought up, and spiritually run down, they became depressed.

Thank God we do not have to stop there. We have seen the *problem*. Now let us look at the . . .

PROVISION

Have you ever thanked God for unanswered prayer? You had better. Wouldn't we be in a mess if God answered "yes" to our foolish prayers, like, "Lord, kill me. Take me home." Believers can pray "amiss" or evilly, as James put it: "Ye ask, and receive not, because ye ask amiss [evilly], that ye may consume it upon your lusts" (3:3). The Holy Spirit helps guard and protect our prayer life.

> Likewise the Spirit also helpeth our infirmities: for we know not what we should pray for as we ought: but the Spirit itself maketh intercession for us with groanings that cannot be uttered (Rom. 8:26).

God does not always give us what we want at the moment but rather what we need.

In dealing with those saints, God in His wisdom did not mistake the moment for the man. He sees all of us in moments of goodness and badness, of weakness and strength. God realized they were going through a bad spell and were submerged in depression.

What did God do for them *physically?* He gave Moses seventy elders to help counsel the people and to settle disputes. God granted him a staff, not merely of wood but of flesh and blood.

> And the Lord said unto Moses, Gather unto me seventy men of the elders of Israel, whom thou knowest to be the elders of the people, and officers over them; and bring them unto the tabernacle of the congregation, that they may stand there with thee (Num. 11:16).

God declared that the elders "shall bear the burden of the people with thee, that thou bear it not thyself alone" (v. 17). God recognized that Moses would break down unless he delegated responsibility. Many people crack up or burn out because they are trying to do too much by themselves. Most of us are going to become worn out physically when we are doing things, no matter how good, God never intended for us to do. To preserve your physical and mental health, you will have to delegate certain tasks and also realize you cannot possibly do all that people ask of you in one day.

Start by making a list of all you are doing that seems so all-fired important. Eliminate some things; delegate others; and then dedicate the rest. *Eliminate, delegate, dedicate.*

God made a physical provision for Moses, but Moses first had to acknowledge his need.

God also made a physical provision for Elijah. After Elijah prayed to die (1 Ki. 19:4) he fell asleep under a juniper tree. Then an angel touched him and said, "Arise and eat" (see vv. 5-6). That is priceless. Elijah asked for death. God gave him dough baked into bread. That's what I call "angel food cake." He also slaked his thirst from a canteen (cruse) at his head. Then he lay down to rest again.

The second time the angel roused him with, "Arise and eat." God knew precisely what Elijah needed, for ahead of him lay a forty-day and forty-night hike to Mount Horeb. At Horeb the prophet entered a cave and stayed awhile ("lodged there," v. 9).

God gave Elijah a period of much-needed rest and recreation (R & R), and then, when the prophet was refreshed in body and mind, God gave him something to do.

David sang that the Lord was his "refuge," which can also mean "resort," a place of rest. Sometimes we ought to, in the words of the spiritual, "Steal away to Jesus." On a number of occasions our Lord Jesus withdrew, sometimes with His disciples, to commune with the Father. His workaholic disciples may have had trouble understanding why Jesus would take time with all the needs around Him.

God recognized that you ought to have a proper, balanced diet and a reasonable amount of rest. You're always running around, wearing yourself thin, breaking down your health. You are not a superman or superwoman. The Bible states that it is vain to stay up late and rise up early. Jesus said repeatedly, "Come apart for awhile." The late Dr. Vance Havner commented, "We had better come apart, or we will come apart." One unnamed philosopher mused, "I have so much to do together, I simply must go to bed."

After Elijah was refreshed, relaxed, and re-created, he was ready for the experience that even topped Mount Carmel. Elijah stood on Horeb . . .

> And, behold, the Lord passed by, and a great and strong wind rent the mountains, and brake in pieces the rocks before the Lord; but the Lord was not in the wind: and after the wind an earthquake; but the Lord was not in the earthquake: And after the earthquake a fire; but the Lord was not in the fire; and after the fire a still small voice (19:11-12).

If Elijah had not calmed down and gone apart, he might never have received this revelation of God's power and character. Through "a still small voice" of His Spirit, God had spoken peace to His depressed servant, and the depression was soon gone.

And how did God deal with Jonah's depression? Jonah sat on the east side of Nineveh and built him a booth (a shed or lean-to). Jonah 4:6 is so revealing about the Lord's provisions.

> And the Lord God prepared a gourd, and made it to come up over Jonah, that it might be a shadow over his head, to deliver him from his grief. So Jonah was exceeding glad of the gourd.

God built Jonah a pastorium and air conditioned it for him. He wanted "to deliver him from his grief." Even though Jonah was still rebellious and harbored hard feelings toward the Ninevites, God caused a luxuriant green vine to provide cover from the blazing sun.

True, God later prepared a worm which killed the gourd. But all that God prepared was for the benefit of Jonah and to rid him from the grief of his depression. Through the gourd God also provided a vivid object lesson—that human beings are worth infinitely more than a gourd vine which soon withers and dies.

What did God do psychologically for these saints? Moses saw *people,* but God gave him a *promise*. "Moses, the battle is the Lord's. Look to Me. I will provide for you." Elijah was afraid of a *woman,* but God showed him a *wonder*. God was in "a still small voice," not in the sound and fury, not in the pyrotechnics. What about moping Jonah? For his petulant *pouting,* God gave him a *perspective*. God had to remove the gourd vine for a while so Jonah could view an entire city out there. God was teaching him, "Get your eyes off of yourself, Son."

Psychologically, God gave all three something far better to take the place of their self-centered introspection. He loved them, brought them back to Himself, and used them. He welcomed them to His bosom.

All kinds of winds blow upon our lives. Fires burn out of control. Pressure. Anxiety. Fear of what may happen. Tune in to God. Go alone with Him in quietness and confidence. Possess your sanity and equilibrium through Him.

If you are given to depression, remember that God wants to deliver you from your grief. He loves you and will never leave you or forsake you. And though people deny Him, He cannot deny Himself. He remains faithful.

These accounts did not end in depression. All three came through. So, even God's choicest servants suffered attacks of depression, but God was always there. They came through . . . and you can, too!

NOTES

1. Nelson L. Price, *Farewell to Fear* (Nashville: Broadman Press, 1983), pp. 109-110.
2. Barbara Taylor, From *Rejection to Acceptance* (Nashville: Broadman Press, 1987), pp. 97-98.

04/26/06

3. Stress Without Distress

Speak through the earthquake, wind and fire,
O still small voice of calm. —Whittier

"A company, concerned about the morale of its top executives, called in a management consultant organization. The report of the results of this organization stunned them. Twenty-one of the twenty-two-man executive committee were suffering from such illnesses as ulcers, high blood pressure, or depression, and their report pointed to one culprit—stress."[1]

"Stress can squeeze years off your life if you don't know how to handle it."[2]

This is the day of the quick cash and the mad dash and what goes with them—stress.

Years ago we may have thought only executives were afflicted with stressful situations, but studies have shown that such unlikely professions as laborer, waitress, machine operator, miner, inspector, painter, hairdresser, meat cutter, plumber, and warehouse worker are fraught with stress. The clergyman is also considered to have a high-stress occupation.

Even the housewives, who may not work outside the home, often have illnesses and breakdowns from stress.

This generation feels it is intelligent, but about all it has added is speed, noise, and pollution. We arrive there faster but still have no idea where we are going, and when we get there, we don't know what to do with ourselves. Someone has observed that this generation can be described in three words—hurry, worry, *bury*.

Americans are becoming hypochondriacs. They consume in the neighborhood of five million pounds of aspirin per year, not counting all of the aspirin-like products, plus sleeping pills, pain pills, pep pills, ad infinitum.

To boot, these stressful conditions are leading to high blood pressure which can result in strokes or aneurysms, runaway heart disease, cancer, and mental illness—and death! The American Heart Association now estimates that fifty-five million American adults—and 2.7 million children—have high blood pressure. In 1985 only thirty-nine million were considered hypertensive.

Many have tried everything else but the most effective remedy, and that is the Bible. This is the Bible's prescription for dealing with stress. Isaiah received this message from the Great Physician:

> Hast thou not known? hast thou not heard, that the everlasting God, the Lord, the Creator of the ends of the earth, fainteth not, neither is weary? There is no searching of his understanding. He giveth power to the faint; and to them that have no might he increaseth strength. Even the youths shall faint and be weary, and the young men shall utterly fall: But they that wait upon the Lord shall renew their strength; they shall mount up with wings as eagles; they shall run, and not be weary; and they shall walk, and not faint. (40:28-31).

First, let us examine . . .

THE PROBLEM OF STRESS

OK. What is the problem of stress? *It is the gap between the demands placed on us and the strength we have in meeting those demands.* Call it what you will—the stress factor, the stress ratio. Over here are the responsibilities, the necessities, the deadlines, the demands, the opportunities—all of those things we want to do, have to do, ought to do, and must do. And over here, seemingly in conflict and pulling in the opposite direction, is my inability, my weakness. I think to myself, *I ought to, I must do, but I can't*. The chasm between all of the ought to's and the seeming can't do's overwhelms me, causing an increasing feeling of frustration and upset. There is an old expression which sums it up: "My can do can't keep up with my want to!"

We used to think of stress in relation to adults, but now young people have more pressures upon them than ever before. There is no excuse for escapism by resorting to drugs and alcohol, but many youths are using them to flee the responsibilities that are thrust upon them. Several years ago we were faced with the "empty-nest syndrome." Now we are amid the phenomenon of the "refeathered-nest syndrome." Finding that they can't or won't cope "out there in the cruel world," many grown children are moving back in with their parents, most of whom are in mid-life or older.

It is not a sin to be stressed, not a sin to be weary, not a sin to run out of strength. It is a sin, though, not to seek a lessening of that stress which tears down the temple of the Holy Spirit, your body.

Now you may be stressful and weary for three basic reasons. Number one, *you may be weary because of the plain demands of service*. Even our Lord and Savior was weary. He understood what it was to be tired. In John 4, Jesus was worn out from His ministry in Judea and was en route to Galilee. "And he must needs go through Samaria" (v. 4). He stopped at Sychar and sat on Jacob's well. He began His witness to "the woman at the well" by asking: "Give me to drink." On foot Jesus had trudged those hot, dusty roads with the Oriental sun beating down on Him. His body was depleted and drained of strength because, not only was (and is) He God, but He was human, yet without sin.

Do you remember Jesus' encounter with the woman who had an issue of blood (chronic hemmorhaging)?

> When she [the woman with the issue of blood] had heard of Jesus, came in the press behind, and touched his garment, For she said, If I

> may touch but his clothes, I shall be whole. And straightway the fountain of her blood was dried up; and she felt in her body that she was healed of the plague. And Jesus, immediately knowing in himself that virtue had gone out of him, turned him about in the press, and said, Who touched my clothes? (Mark 5:27-30).

"Virtue had gone out of him" means that power and strength had left His body, and He could sense it. Miraculously His power was transferred to heal her malady. His strength became her strength and healing.

I cannot understand the full impact of this spiritual truth, but when you serve, when you minister, strength goes out from you. Your life is spent. John the Baptist was called a burning and shining light. There can be no shining without burning, and when you burn, you are consumed. The pathway of service can deplete your stamina and strength.

No doubt you recall when Jesus was so tired He fell asleep in a boat on the Sea of Galilee. "And, behold, there arose a great tempest in the sea . . . but he was asleep" (Matt. 8:24). Jesus was asleep not only to give the disciples an example of His calm amid a storm, but also because He was bone tired. There was not a lazy fiber in His body—He was simply tired. "Even the youths shall faint and be weary," wrote Isaiah.

Quite frankly I have never known a servant of the Lord Jesus, one who was dedicated and conscientious, who was not worn out a considerable amount of time. As you serve God, as you do what He and others call upon you to do, your strength will be sapped. "Virtue" will emanate from you, yet your duties will remain. The chasm between your duties and the energy you have left to do them will result in frustration and stress. And you will ask yourself repeatedly, *How am I going to do it? How can I function? How can I possibly live up to others' expectations?*

Not only the *demands of service,* but also the *dissipation of sin,* will drain the strength from you. The demands of service are good; the dissipation of sin is bad.

Samson was the heavyweight champion of the Old Testament. He was perhaps the strongest man in history. With his bare hands he destroyed a lion as though it were a baby goat; he carried off the iron gates of Gaza on his broad shoulders; he wiped out an army of the heathen Philistines with the jawbone of a jackass as his only weapon, but he was weak of character. The dissipation of sin set in, and the *devices of the devil* began to steal his strength. He started having an affair with a Philistine harlot, Delilah. He prostituted his relationship with God. Because of his sin he had the most expensive haircut in history as Delilah learned the secret of his power symbolized by his long Nazarite hair. While he was asleep in her lap she barbered him and gave the signal for the Philistines to rush in and capture him. Sin had made him as puny as a newborn mouse.

The dissipation of sin drains physical, emotional, moral, and spiritual strength. All of that is compounded by the *devices of Satan*.

Satan often waits until you are weary to oppose you spiritually. Many a Christian falls prey to the devil by neglecting his health, by burning the proverbial candle at both ends, by eating poorly, and failing to have enough rest and sleep. Maybe the expression, "I'd rather burn out than rust out," sounds pious, but servants of Christ often use it as an excuse to abuse their God-given bodies.

> Remember what Amalek did unto thee by the way, when we were come forth out of Egypt; How he met thee, even all that were feeble behind thee, when thou wast faint and weary; and he feared not God (Deut. 25:17-18).

God wanted the Israelites to remember the perfidy of wicked King Amalek. Moses reminded the people that Amalek attacked the nation when it was enervated and vulnerable. The Amalekites sneaked up on the Israelites' rear where the handicapped, feeble, and weak followed. He did it when the children of Israel were exhausted in their flight from Egypt.

None of us are immune from stress. "Even the youths shall faint." Even the grammar-school child is under stress from his schoolmates. Today he may actually fear harm from bullies, failure in his courses, disappointing his parents. And the highest rate of suicide in America is among youth and young adults, ages 18-21! Stress stalks our steps.

But stress does not need to defeat you. Now, in addition to *the problem of stress,* I want you to notice . . .

THE PROMISE OF STRENGTH

Verse 31 bears repeating:

> But they that wait upon the Lord shall renew their strength; they shall mount up with wings as eagles; they shall run, and not be weary; and they shall walk and not faint.

"They that wait upon the Lord shall renew their strength." Renew is from the Hebrew word *chaleth,* which literally means "they shall exchange their strength." The Christian life is not only a changed life but also *an exchanged one*. I give Him my strength, which is really weakness, and even then, "the weakness of God is stronger than men" (1 Cor. 1:25*b*). The Lord advised Paul, "My grace is sufficient for thee: for my strength is made perfect in weakness" (2 Cor. 12:9).

Galatians 2:20 describes the case of the exchanged life: "I am crucified with Christ: nevertheless I live; yet not I, but Christ liveth in me: and the life which I now in the flesh I live by the faith of the Son of God who loved me, and gave himself for me." The crucified life is not only a changed life but an exchanged life.

Now, the question arises, How do you wait upon the Lord? because this is the crux of the entire matter. I firmly believe this is the answer to stress.

The key to dealing with stress is in this little phrase: "wait upon the Lord."

The Psalmist wrote almost the same words in Psalm 27:14: "Wait on the Lord: be of good courage, and he shall strengthen thine heart: wait, I say, on the Lord."

"Hold it," you might interrupt, "what do you mean by *wait?*" How often Christians miss the thrust of *wait*. Most think that waiting on the Lord is a form of passivity, sitting around anticipating that God is going to do this or that. Actually, it is not passivity—it is *activity*.

This may contradict all you ever heard about this text, but waiting on the Lord implies initiative, not only God's but yours as well. Years ago when a fellow courted a girl, they called it "waiting" on her. Sometimes it meant literally waiting on her because she was late! Ahem. But it meant that he was pursuing her, going after her, head over heels in love with her. When you are waiting on God, you are really pursuing Him with all your being, wanting to please Him and to serve Him. In other words, you want to be at His "beck and call." Waiting on God.

Here I want to quote four Scripture verses which use the word *wait*. If waiting upon God is the secret of strength, then by all means you need to learn how to wait upon God.

First, wait indicates that *you are to long for the Lord*. You need to have a deep-down desire in your heart for the Lord.

Psalm 62:1 . . . "Truly my soul waiteth upon God: from him cometh my salvation."

It reminds me of the chorus we used to sing: "Longing, longing for Jesus, I have a longing in my heart for Him, Just to be near Him, To feel His presence, I have a longing in my heart for Him." We need to long, to pine, to yearn for close fellowship with Him. "As the hart [young deer] pants after the water brooks, so panteth my soul after thee, O God" (Ps. 42:1).

To wait upon God is to long for Him, to desire Him. Then, second of all, if you long for Him, *you will listen to Him*.

Proverbs 8:34 . . . "Blessed is the man that heareth me, watching daily at my gates, waiting at the posts of my doors." Here God links waiting with listening, not only hearing but heeding. "Watching daily at my gates" carries with it the idea that we are to be His butlers, his doormen. We are to have a daily assignment from God and an appointment with Him. I believe this means a quiet time with Him when we can commune with Him in meditation and prayer. *The answer to stress is a quiet time with God.*

So many of us are "all shook up" because we have not met God in the morning, noon, or night. Many people have an almost nonexistent prayer life.

We believe so many things absolutely have to be done, and, in addition, we do so many things because they are prompted by our secret motives, that our days and our lives are too short. It does not follow that one first should fulfill his duty, then satisfy his own desires, and finally in the time that remains, listen to God. Generally not much time is left. It should be the other way around. First listen to God and place in His hands our entire lives.

We talk and preach about this quiet time but seldom practice it. No wonder we are filled with stress if we seldom seek God's face, seldom saturate our souls in the Word, and seldom bathe ourselves in His presence.

To wait upon God means to *long* for Him; then we *listen* to Him . . . *then we learn to look to Him.*

Psalm 104:27 . . . "These wait all upon thee; that thou mayest give them their meat in due season." In this Psalm the psalmist is praising God's provisions in nature. He has sung of the wild asses, the fowls of the heaven, the cattle, birds in general, the stork, the night beasts of the forest, the young lion cubs, creatures of the sea including the leviathan, all of these on land, sea, and in the air. All of these creatures look to God for their sustenance.

Our Lord Jesus carried out this theme throughout His ministry. "Behold the fowls of the air: for they sow not, neither do they reap, nor gather into barns; yet your heavenly Father feedeth them. Are ye not much better than they?" (Matt. 6:26). Looking to God means you are fully dependent on Him. You are well aware: "Lord, I cannot live without You. I am not self-reliant but 100 percent reliant on You." Like the old Gospel song, "Where could I go but to the Lord?"

> Ye fearful saints, fresh courage take;
> The clouds ye so much dread
> Are big with mercy, and shall break
> In blessings on your head.
>
> —William Cowper

Long for Him. Listen to Him. Look to Him . . . and *live for him,*

Proverbs 27:18 . . . "Whoso keepeth the fig tree shall eat the fruit thereof: so he that waiteth on his master shall be honoured."

How do you keep a fig tree? Many folks in the Deep South still have fig trees. To many of us there is nothing like fig preserves on hot biscuits. To keep a fig tree you do not merely sit out in the back yard and watch it. You prune it, fertilize it, water it, nurture it. You protect it from blight and insect pests. The principle here is: if you want the produce, you have to pay the price. Then you have a right to eat the luscious fruit. By the same token the person who waits on his Master is going to be honored and recognized.

Living for Him indicates that we will care for His cause even with more diligence than we would tending to our fruit trees. When a person serves God, He may expect heavenly fruit.

Recently they have changed the term waiter or waitress to server, and that is closer to this idea. We wait on the Lord, but that entails serving Him.

Thousands of dedicated believers are serving with little or no distinction. In this warring world, which daily cringes from the threat of terrorism, our missionaries are exposing themselves to torture and death in order to wait upon Jesus. Especially in the Middle East and Africa, missionaries are being imprisoned, threatened, and murdered. As I write this book, I am reading of an estimated one thousand Christians who were massacreed in the Sudan by terrorists. Why? Because they served and waited on Jesus. Only a few weeks ago a number of

Christians in Zimbabwe were hacked to death by revolutionaries.

Waiting on the Lord demands "my life, my soul, my all." When we learn to wait on Him, God steps in to bridge the stress factor with His mighty strength.

We have dealt with the *problem of stress* and *the promise of strength*—and now . . .

THE PROGRAM OF SERVICE

"They that wait upon the Lord shall renew their strength." What happens? First of all, "they shall mount up with wings as eagles." Second, "they shall run, and not be weary." Third, "they shall walk and not faint."

I have in mind three factors which cause stress: *adversity,* the storms of life; *opportunity,* what we want to do but we are afraid those desires and dreams will elude us; and *necessity,* what we have to do, must do. All of these are stressors.

Adversity comes upon us unexpectedly. We did not program ourselves for the storms of life. We do not want adversity unless we are mentally ill. Opportunity is embodied in those dreams ahead of us. Yet, we are afraid we cannot seize those opportunities. At the same time, many people even fear success because of the pressure and responsibility it could involve. Necessities are those tasks we have to do or must do to keep going, to earn a living, to satisfy certain demands upon us.

If we have difficulty in any of these areas, we will experience stress.

Strength in Adversity.

Think for a moment about adversity. From what I have learned about the eagle, he thrives in altitudes. The eagle also seems to long for the storm, because those thermal underdrafts of the storm cause him to soar higher and higher than he could have prior to the storm. The storm is no longer a threat to him because he spreads those powerful wings and glides above the ink-black storm clouds beneath him.

First, the storm compels him to fly higher and farther and faster. Normally an eagle can fly fifty miles an hour, but in a storm eagles have been clocked at almost one hundred miles an hour. Those very turbulent winds that would defeat others make him do his utmost, because God engineered him for the storm.

All of us are going to be buffeted by adversities and the storms of life. Those storms are going to stretch you and rack you unless you are waiting on the Lord. But if you wait on God, He is going to give you strength for weakness. Because God will afford you strength for elevation, you are going to rise above those treacherous underdrafts.

Strength for Opportunity.

Think for a moment about *opportunity*. God is not only going to provide you strength for *elevation* but also power for *acceleration*. Not only will you spiritually mount up with wings as eagles, but you "shall run, and not be weary."

Opportunities will arise, and we will have to move quickly. A person who is serving God is going to have constant deadlines. How well I know! I can understand why they call due dates, deadlines. Sometimes you will feel dead as you try to meet those expectations and schedules.

Day by day demands are placed upon me. Deadlines are coming at me thick and fast. Sometimes I feel as though I am at the end of the runway but have not left the ground. Adrian, it's time to preach, to meet, to plan, etc., etc., etc. I preach at least six times a week, sometimes ten and twelve times a week. And I do not want to miss the opportunities for Christ. I do not want to fail, and I have to run. It reminds me of verse three of "The Battle Hymn of the Republic": "O be swift, my soul, to answer Him; be jubilant, my feet! Our God is marching on."

Philip the deacon is a prime example of a servant who grabbed opportunity without questioning. He was waiting on the Lord, and the angel instructed him to go out into the desert which is now called the Gaza Strip. You are familiar with the account. Philip acted and led the Ethiopian eunuch to the Lord. Philip went at the precise moment (see Acts 8:26-39). Had he argued with the angel of the Lord, he would have missed an unparalleled opportunity.

I once read about a sign on a barrel of fish: "If not delivered in three days, never mind." Philip did not wait. And tradition tells us that the eunuch opened up all of North Africa to the Gospel.

Walter Malone wrote a poem that speaks volumes:

They do me [opportunity] wrong
who say I come no more
When once I knock and fail to
find you in,
For every day I stand outside
your door
And bid you wake, and rise to
fight and win.

. . . .

Art thou a mourner? Rouse thee
from thy spell;
Art thou a sinner? Sins may
be forgiven;
Each morning gives thee wings
to flee from hell,
Each night a star to guide thy
feet to Heaven.

When you are confronted with opportunities, and you do not have the strength to respond, you had better spend time waiting on the Lord. The other day a friend shared a truth that put me under conviction. "No one should ever attempt to do more than he can pray over." That is sound counsel. Yet many fail to do what they can do.

Strength in Necessity.

Adversity, opportunity, and now *necessity*. The sage was right: "Necessity is the mother of invention." Sometimes the necessities seem the worst. I *have* to clean the house. I *have* to go to the office. I *have* to punch the clock. Why? Because I *have* to have a semblance of order in my life . . . because my family and I *have* to eat, wear clothes, live in a home, and—if possible—*have* a vehicle. The necessities. Sometimes we want to do them, sometimes not.

In verse 31 God is saving the best for the last. "Mount up with wings as eagles," "run, and not be weary," and now "walk and not faint." Not only elevation and acceleration but now *determination*. We can soar, we can run, but more often than not we will have to live with the pedestrian side of life.

What is victorious Christian living? Many think, *Why, it's becoming an international evangelist, a "celebrity," or a missionary martyr*. However, it is not soaring like an eagle or running like a deer. It's really fixing breakfast, dressing the kids for school, sending them off with a kiss, and still praising Jesus.

It's typing those letters with a smile on your face. It's mopping floors and taking out the garbage. It's mundane, ordinary living. So many Christians have complained, "My life's dull and uninteresting. There's no glamour. I wish I could leave what I'm doing and be famous like Billy Graham or . . ." Maybe our best service is *to walk day by day*. If God wants us to soar and run, He will enable us.

Waiting on the Lord is "following Jesus one step at a time." "One day at a time, sweet Jesus." It's serving God in good days and bad, hot days and cold, every day, in every way, day after day, night after night, week after week, month after month, year after year—*walking* in Jesus.

One preacher called our day-by-day walk "religion in shoe leather." More of us fall flat on our faces doing the necessity when we are simply walking, than when we are in adversity or opportunity. It is a thrilling matter to have soaring power and surging power. But it is more necessary to have sticking, staying power, "to walk and faint not," to keep on keeping on for Jesus.

What is the answer to stress? "Wait upon the Lord." Long for the Lord. Listen to Him. Look to Him. Live for Him. It sounds simplistic. Right? But it works. It really does!

NOTES

1. John W. Drakeford, *The Awesome Power of the Healing Thought* (Nashville: Broadman Press, 1981). pp. 17-18.
2. Ibid., p. 17.

4. Detours, Dead Ends, and Dry Holes

For while the tired waves, vainly breaking,
Seem here no painful inch to gain,
Far back, through creeks and inlets making,
Comes silent, flooding in, the main.
—Arthur Hugh Clough

Frustration is a word often mispronounced. It is often mistakenly called "flustration" or "flusteration." Whatever one names it, frustration is a destructive emotion.

What is it? Most of us have a fairly accurate idea. It is the emotion of conflict which courses through our systems, making us miffed, causing us to breath heavily and turn red in the face. Our blood pressure rises, and our hearts race. The anger attached with frustration is our systems trying to react against a seemingly impossible barrier.

One country comedian aptly summed it up, "It makes me so mad I could eat a goat burger!" Frustration is the upset of not being able to succeed, sometimes because of implausible reasons. Frustration was the emotion experienced by the young women of the mythical kingdom who tried to force their shovel-like feet into Cinderella's tiny glass slipper. Frustration would be, in the words of Roger Miller, trying to take a shower in a parakeet cage or endeavoring to roller skate in a buffalo herd.

Frustration is harmful to the system because it means the dashing of hopes and dreams, the inability to reach a goal, and the disappointing embarrassment of failure. Frustration is experienced by the Little League benchwarmer who has been promised a time at bat by the coach only to have him renege at the last minute and send in another batter. Frustration is missing your next plane at Chicago's O'Hare Field because your plane made an unannounced stop in Kansas City to pick up eleven well-heeled passengers, causing you not to make an extremely important meeting in another city. Frustration is when you "try, try again," and nothing seems to succeed.

The Book of Hebrews has three thrilling chapters that help us to face frustration. They tell of God's dealing with His ancient people on their journey from bondage in Egypt to fulfillment in Canaan. God makes it clear in the New Testament that their experience can be used for "examples to us" (1 Cor. 10:11).

All of us are on a journey, as were the children of Israel. When we were saved, we began that journey. The wilderness wanderings of the Israelites are lessons for us today. We can profit from their experiences.

THE DISCIPLINE OF DETOURS

> And it came to pass, when Pharaoh had let the people go, that God led them not through the way of the land of the Philistines, although that was near; for God said, Lest peradventure the people repent when they see war, and they return to Egypt (Ex. 13:17).

What are the implications of this pivotal verse? Many have mistakenly thought that the children of Israel followed their "circuitous route" through their own choosing. That was not at all the case. "God led them not through the way of the land of Philistines." Yes, God led them, but He knew what was best for them. The Heavenly Father does know best.

As the crow flies, the route to Canaan from Egypt was through Philistea. "Although that was near." God was protecting them from the danger of war at this time; he did not want them to hightail it and return to the bondage of Egypt.

God led them on a back road, if indeed there was any road, in the middle of nowhere. They traveled around and around in circles because it was His providential plan. This is a prime lesson: God did not want them to get there, to "arrive," too quickly.

Youth is marvelous, and I am grateful for young servants of the Lord. But there is a danger that they will not have the proper seasoning in the wilderness before possessing the Promised Land. I often pray for my younger preacher brethren, "Lord, help them not to get there too fast and be defeated early." It is easy to get in over one's head.

So, God did not want the Hebrews over in the Promised Land until the time He had appointed. One of the pitfalls of youth is overzealous enthusiasm, a zeal not according to knowledge. The Hebrews were on a seemingly not-so-merry-go-round. They were short sighted, but God envisioned the long haul. Only He can see all of eternity in one glance.

> But God led the people about, through the way of the wilderness of the Red Sea: and the children of Israel went up harnessed out of the land of Egypt (Ex. 13:18).

He led them about, around in circles. Why? He certainly did it to test and try them—also to toughen them. There is no blessing without a battle. God wanted them to pick their battles carefully. Paul's statement concerning the warfare is helpful: "For we wrestle not against flesh and blood, but against principalities, against powers, against the rulers of the darkness of this world, against spiritual wickedness in high places" (Eph. 6:12).

We may think, *Hmmm, going around in circles. It sounds like me. I seem to be going nowhere in a hurry. Why can't I progress?* You may even feel at times that God has forsaken you.

If you love Christ, if you long to please Him, remember this: *God's delays are not God's denials*. Many a Christian feels he is out in the wilderness; all he is doing is being led "about," in circles. I can remember years ago when I wanted instant progress. I desired it at an early age, but God has His own timetable.

When I was nineteen years old and in college, one of my friends reported that he was going to see Dr. Robert G. Lee, for years the pastor of Bellevue Baptist Church. Every Baptist preacher boy virtually agreed that Dr. Lee was the greatest preacher since New Testament days. He was synonymous with powerful preaching that wafted you to heaven.

I could not believe my ears when this friend came back and announced, "I had a visit with Dr. R. G. Lee." I asked him how he managed that (I have to admit I was a mite envious), and he said, "I went to his secretary and asked if I could see him." Good grief, I could not imagine a pastor having a secretary—maybe the church having one but not the pastor. He went on, "The secretary ushered me in."

"What did you do?" I inquired. "Oh, we talked a while. He asked about me, and then he had prayer for me." I was amazed.

I was on the backside of the desert, going in circles out in the wilderness. I was bashful and timid. I didn't have the brass to walk in and visit with Dr. Lee. Years later Bellevue Baptist Church called me as their pastor. I became pastor of that same church!

Shortly after I had settled in as pastor, my secretary informed me, "Dr. Lee is out here, and he'd like to see you."

Maybe God is grooming you. He is not ready to thrust you into heavy responsibilities as yet. He has you in a holding pattern. Those circles are for a specific purpose.

God was working in my life at the time. Sometimes I was not able to recognize His hand. I can remember one little church where I had to clean and sweep the building before we could meet. I was the pastor, janitor, and general flunkey, and that was OK. It does not matter if you are on what seems to be a back road, if God is with you. In the words of the old hymn, "If Jesus goes with me, I'll go anywhere."

The detours may not thrill you, but they will test you. God is aware that if He pushes you straight on through, you might fall flat on your face. The Philistines are out there, and you might not be able to face them now. One day you will be ready but not right this moment. God does not want you to panic and run back toward Egypt.

God will give us guidance, even if it is a detour. How did He do it?

> And the Lord went before them by day in a pillar of cloud, to lead them the way; and by night in a pillar of fire, to give them light; to go by day and night (Ex. 13:21).

To me the pillar of cloud by day and the pillar of fire by night represent the presence of the Holy Spirit. The shekinah glory of God was shining upon them as they wandered in the wilderness. God will not leave you guideless in the detour periods of your life. The Holy Spirit is the Paraclete, one Who accompanies us and goes alongside us. He is "constantly abiding" . . . "I will never leave thee," Jesus promises.

The Spirit is in you, He surrounds you, He goes before you, with you, and beside you. Exodus 13:22 is assuring: "He took not away the pillar of the cloud by day, nor the pillar of fire by night, from before the people." He took not away the pillar of fire and the pillar of cloud. That is true on the back road or on the boulevard.

You must keep in sight the pillar of cloud and the pillar of fire. You need to live in the continual, conscious presence of God. You may not always have a road map, but you have a *relationship* in Christ. You need to exemplify in your life, "Nothing between my soul and the Saviour."

You are on the journey. Paul was always aware of it. "Not as though I had already attained, either were already perfect; but I follow after, if that I may apprehend that for which also I am apprehended of Christ Jesus. Brethren, I count not myself to have apprehended: but this one thing I do, forgetting those things which are behind, and reaching forth unto those those which are before" (Phil. 3:12-13).

You have not arrived. You have not reached Canaan. God has His own timetable for you. You are "pressing on the upward way." There is a Gospel song that fractures grammar, but it carries a message: "I wouldn't take nothing for my journey now." You are a pilgrim and a stranger in a barren, wilderness land. All you need to know is to know that you know Him.

God leads you through the wilderness and the detours because He is preparing something wonderful for you, something better. He doesn't want you to settle for less than His optimum for your life and your work.

I have heard of an evangelist whose wife died, leaving him with two little boys to rear. He hired a woman to stay with them while he was in his crusades. When he traveled, he would nearly always return with presents for the boys. One particular flight, though, he forgot to buy their gifts.

"Daddy, Daddy," they shouted as they met him at the airport. Of course, they asked him about the presents. He said, "Boys, what we're going to do is let you get anything you want." So they stopped at a large store. First, they went by the candy counter. They wanted candy, but their daddy suggested they keep looking. They came to two cowboy suits with the toy guns, hat, and lariat. The boys wanted to settle on the suits. Daddy asked them to look further.

They moved farther back into the store to the sporting goods. The boys picked up basketballs and began to dribble, "Daddy, Daddy, we want these basketballs." They were excited. Finally, they went all the way back, and against the wall were two shiny bicycles—a Comet and a Silver Streak. The boys left with far more than they bargained for. They started with candy and ended up with expensive bikes that Daddy had wanted to buy all the time.

Frustrated? Sometimes that is why you have to keep moving on. God has something marvelous for you out there—after the detours, after the wilderness. God is not leading you around in circles for no reason. You'll see.

First, there is the *discipline of detours*. Then there is . . .

THE DILEMMA OF DEAD ENDS

And the Lord hardened the heart of Pharaoh king of Egypt, and he

> pursued after the children of Israel: and the children of Israel went out with a high hand. But the Egyptians pursued after them, all the horses and chariots of Pharaoh, and his horsemen, and his army, and overtook them encamping by the sea, beside Pihahiroth, before Baalzephon. And when Pharaoh drew nigh, the children of Israel lifted up their eyes, and, behold, the Egyptians marched after them; and they were sore afraid: and the children of Israel cried out unto the Lord (Ex. 14:8-10).

First, there was the *discipline of detours*. Now they were met with *the dilemma of dead ends*, and what a dead end! They were brought to a cul de sac, a total dead end. They were camped by the sea, and the terrain prohibited their escape. Pharaoh's army was closing in on them. For those who never read the Book there was also a movie!

"And they said unto Moses, Because there were no graves in Egypt, hast thou taken us away to die in the wilderness? wherefore hast thou dealt thus with us, to carry us forth out of Egypt?" (Ex. 14:11). Then they continued their lament. "We said, 'Let us alone, that we may serve the Egyptians, for that is better than dying in the wilderness'" (see v. 12).

What the children of Israel did not know, or seem to know, was that all of this was by divine design. In this chapter, verses 1-4, God explained what was happening. Pharaoh and his army would ride into a trap. God explained, "I will be honoured upon Pharaoh, and upon all his host; that the Egyptians may know that I am the Lord. And they did so" (v. 4).

Even though the situation seemed impossible, God put the Israelites exactly where He wanted them. And He also had Pharaoh and his host precisely where He wanted them.

As it were God was baiting the hook of judgment for Pharaoh. Pharaoh had hardened his heart repeatedly and would not listen to Moses the servant of Jehovah. 1. God baited the hook. 2. God was planning something magnificent for the children of Israel.

Once I had the rare opportunity of visiting with Corrie ten Boom, who is now in heaven. I drank in her words. I listened and kept my mouth shut. One of her statements went straight to my heart: "There is no panic in heaven, only plans." That is how God operates. No panic. Only plans.

But the people of Israel were panicking. From every standpoint they were goners. Hear this. The Holy Trinity never has to meet in "emergency session."

You may be in a seemingly bad shape right now. The enemy, to use an old cliché, seems to be "beating you around a stump." Did you ever stop to think that God was preparing you for His magnificence and might? You are surrounded on all sides, but remember the pillar of cloud by day and the pillar of fire by night. If you are in the wilderness it is for a reason.

Moses reassured the people.

> And Moses said unto the people, Fear ye not, stand still, and see the salvation of the Lord, which he will show to you today: for the Egyptians whom ye have seen today, ye shall see them again no more for ever (v. 13).

In all of these situations you are to *refuse fear* and you are to *renew faith*. You have a divine appointment. The Israelites were backed almost into the sea, and the Egyptians were catching up with them. Terror was sweeping across the camp. They were at their extremity. I have always loved Spurgeon's maxim: "Man's extremity is God's opportunity."

What a reassurance! "Fear not. Stand still, and see the salvation [the deliverance] of the Lord." The term "fear not" is used in one form or another 365 times in the Word of God, one for each day of the year. "Fear thou not." They were not to have a spirit of fear, a fear that would blind them and render them helpless and weak.

When I pastored in Merritt Island, Florida, we were in a building program. One afternoon I decided to walk across the street and look at the educational buildings. I walked into one of the buildings, and the door closed behind me. To my chagrin I found that the room I had entered had no knob on the door and no windows. It was awfully dark in there. Then I felt the presence of someone else in there with me.

I called out, "May I help you?" Sometimes that may mean, "What are you doing here?" which was my next question. Then I dimly saw a man—about six inches taller than I and big! My heart began to pound, my hands began to sweat, and I prayed for more light. I decided, *Oh well, I might as well be brave.* So, I moved toward him, and he moved toward me. Oh, oh. Something was going to have to give. Then I recognized him. Guess who the big guy was. Me! There was a big glass mirror across the room, and I had been looking at myself.

When I found out who he was—namely me—he wasn't nearly as big and ugly as I had thought. I was afraid because of a distorted image—fear. If we are in the Spirit, God brings us to the place where we must hear His "fear not." "Stand still, and see the salvation of God." God brings us to *the point of desperation* that He might bring us to *the point of dependence* that He might finally bring us to *the point of deliverance*. Through that God gets the glory.

It is frustrating to roam around in the wilderness, to wait, seemingly to mark time, even to "stand still." It was even worse because now the Israelites felt they were doomed for sure. *The discipline of a detour* seemed grievous to them, and many finally died in the wilderness. The detour, for the most part, was boring. But *the dilemma of a dead end* could mean death, instant death, not death over a long period of time, as had been the case when they had wandered in circles.

But you are familiar with what God did. He opened up a forty-eight-lane superhighway through the Red Sea. God did what many try to disclaim or dispute. If there is a God, and there is, He is the greatest miracle of all. Since He exists, anything is possible if He desires it. I could never understand how a Christian could refuse to believe in the miracles of God's Word. God divided the waters of the Red Sea, "and the children of Israel went into the midst of the sea upon the dry land: and the waters were a wall unto them on their right hand, and on their left. And the Egyptians pursued, and went in after them to the midst of the sea, even all Pharaoh's horses, his chariots, and his horsemen" (Ex. 14:23-24). The Egyptians followed the bait.

The Israelites' dead end was turned into a departure from danger. Verse 27 declares: "And all the host of Pharaoh that came into the sea after them; there remained not so much as one of them." They were drowned in the Red Sea.

The *discipline of detours, the dilemma of dead ends,* and now . . .

THE DISAPPOINTMENT OF DRY HOLES

You would think that the people would have been ecstatic over the Exodus from Egypt and the deliverance through the Red Sea—but no. They were typical Baptists. Start reading in chapter 15:

> So Moses brought Israel from the Red Sea, and they went out into the wilderness of Shur; and they went three days in the wilderness, and found no water. And when they came to Marah, they could not drink of the waters of Marah, for they were bitter: therefore the name of it was called Marah. And the people murmured against Moses, saying, What shall we drink? (Ex. 15:22-24).

God had led them all the way. He wanted to prove and to test them. Yet, they were not out of the will of God. It was His purpose for them to be in the wilderness. They were led there by the pillar of cloud and the pillar of fire to a dry hole. And why? It was a test. "There he proved [tested] them" (v. 25). But they failed the test.

It reminds me of the college man who complained to his professor, "Dr., I don't deserve this F." To which the professor replied, "I know it, young man, but we don't have a grade any lower than an F."

Shortly before the journey to Marah, the people had celebrated their deliverance with song and dance. Moses had been a hero who had gone to zero.

Let this compute. In 1 Corinthians 10:7-10 God ranks murmuring with adultery and fornication as one of the most grievous sins. "And the people murmured against Moses, saying, What shall we drink?"

(v. 24). "Do all things without murmuring," Paul advised. No matter what, we are not to murmur against God and those He has placed in the roles of spiritual leadership. Murmuring is rooted in vicious unbelief.

Murmurers in the church are a hindrance to the cause of Christ. I heard about a church member who complained all the time. He constantly snooped around the church, and one day he opened a closet door to find five brooms. He was outraged and began to ask where the brooms came from and what they were doing there. He complained to the pastor who in turn went to the treasurer. "Oh," answered the treasurer, "it's easy to see. He hates to see his total giving for last year tied up in five brooms." Murmuring is a deadly sin, and many of the murmurers did later die in the wilderness.

> And he [Moses] cried unto the Lord; and the Lord showed him a tree, which when he had cast into the waters, the waters were made sweet. There he made for them a statute and an ordinance, and there he proved them (v. 25).

The tree had been there all the time. To me that tree speaks of the Cross. It was there to sweeten bitter waters. And the Cross sweetens all of life. "Jesus is the sweetest name I know." But the Cross must be applied by faith to life's bitter experiences.

Does God have a sense of humor? The Hebrews were complaining and just over the hill—a few sand dunes away—was an oasis.

> And they came to Elim, where were twelve wells of water, and three score and ten palm trees: and they encamped there by the waters (v. 27).

Aleksandr Solzhenitsyn, the brilliant Russian literary genius, was imprisoned for his political and religious convictions. He was cut off from all contact with the outside world—no letters, newspapers, or conversation. He was put to grueling labor. What a dry hole!

The suffering took its toll. Solzhenitsyn contemplated suicide, but his faith would not allow it. Then, his mind distracted by the situation, conceived this plan. "I will run in an attempted escape. They will shoot me, but it will not be suicide." The guard was there with his rifle.

Solzhenitsyn was ready to spring up and run when a fellow prisoner came and stood before him. Solzhenitsyn later said, "He looked into my eyes as if he could read my every thought." Remember they were not allowed to speak. Then, with a stick as if he were merely doodling, this unknown prisoner drew a cross in the dirt.

Solzhenitsyn said, "I knew he was a messenger from God and that what I was doing was wrong. I settled down to trust God." Little did Solzhenitsyn know that in a few days he would be a free man in Switzerland.

God showed him a tree, and right over the hill was his oasis.

Remember this when you come to a dry hole. Not only is Jesus necessary, He is enough, but as we will see in a later chapter, we may never learn that He is enough until He is all we have!

In your journey God will turn every heartache to a hallelujah, every tear to a pearl, every desert to an oasis, and every Calvary to Easter!

5. God's Hall of Fame

But the man who fails and yet fights on,
Lo! he is the twin-born brother of mine!
—Joaquin Miller

For as long as I can remember I have heard about so-called "inferiority complexes." And inferiority is exactly that—complex. Psychologists even claim that the "superiority complex" is actually a facade for feelings of inferiority.

No doubt you heard about the fellow who was obsessed with feelings of inferiority. He finally consulted a psychiatrist and visited him for consultation over a period of months at the cost of thousands of dollars. At long last the psychiatrist rocked the client back on his heels. "Mr. Jones," the doctor intoned in a professional air, "I have discovered the root of your problem. You're just plain inferior!"

Many of us feel inferior, no count, helpless—and seldom do our friends or families seem to help. One preacher allegedly asked his wife at breakfast, "Honey, how many really great preachers do you think are in the world?"

"I don't know," she countered, "But there's probably one less than you think there are." What a letdown!

So, we are often down in the dumps about our emotions, about our seeming uselessness, inability, and immobility. In fact, Christians all too often think they are "no earthy good for heaven's sake." As it were, we pout and sulk, moaning to ourselves the lyrics of a song, "You're no good, you're no good, Baby, you're no good!"

His writings to the Corinthians have bearing on this matter of inferiority.

> For ye see your calling, brethren, how that not many wise men after the flesh, not many mighty, not many noble, are called: But God hath chosen the weak things of the world to confound the things which are mighty; And base things of the world, and things which are despised, hath God chosen, yea, and things which are not, to bring to nought things that are; That no flesh should glory in his presence. But of him are ye in Christ Jesus, who of God is made unto us wisdom, and righteousness, and sanctification, and redemption: That, according as it is written, He that glorieth, let him glory in the Lord (1 Cor. 1:26-31).

In my own church I asked for a show of hands. "How many are athletes—All Conference, All American, and the like?" A few hands were raised. "Then how many of you have earned doctor's degrees?" Several hands were lifted. "Miss America, Miss Tennessee, Miss World, Miss Universe?" Very few hands. Quite a few had been college or high school class presidents and "Most Likely to Succeed" and "Who's Who."

Then, with a smile on my face, I said, "Then I have wonderful news for you. God can use you, too, but He may have to work a little harder to do it."

The fact is that most of us are ordinary people. The truth I offer to all of you is: God uses ordinary people who have seemingly pedestrian lives, and He does an extraordinary work in them. Through it He is glorified.

All you have to do is scrutinize the apostles, for instance. Fishermen, a tax collector, a "zealot." None of them had sat at the feet of the more learned rabbis. What a ragtag bunch, but they ended up "turning the world upside down." And those who watched them exclaimed, "Why, these are ignorant and unlearned men!" But the

Scripture notes, "They took knowledge of them that they had been with Jesus" (see Acts 4:13). First, I want you to look at . . .

GOD'S SIMPLE PEOPLE

That's right. Simple. Common. Plain. Ordinary. "But God hath chosen the foolish things of the world to confound [shame] the wise; and God hath chosen the weak things of the world to confound the things which are mighty" (v. 27).

That word "foolish" is derived from the Greek word *moros*. Notice the similarity to "moron." It comes from the same root and literally means non-intellectual. It refers to those who were considered "dummies" by the world. Paul was trying to demonstrate the usability of all sorts of people, not merely the intelligentsia.

God can even use the seemingly dumb to mystify those who are considered brilliant. This is not a put-down. It is merely a statement of fact that God can use anyone. Those who feel inadequate and even stupid can be more successful in life because they are aware of their limitations—and therefore depend on God all the more.

No doubt it is a superb honor to be intellectual and belong to the organization of geniuses called Mensa. But God realized that most of His creatures would be what we call in the country, "fair to middling." Nothing extraordinary, nothing spectacular, nothing exceptional. Most of us, to cite an old ballad, "are just plain folks, plain as any folks could be."

"And God hath chosen the weak things of the world to confound the things which are mighty" (v. 27*b*). Weak literally means those who are physically weak—the anemic, the emaciated, the puny. How can God do that?

"And base things of the world, and things which are despised, hath God chosen, yea, and things which are not, to bring to nought things that are" (v. 28). "Base carries with it the idea of worse than lowly—in other words, a zilch, a cipher, of no consideration at all. Zero!

In this context "the base things" mean low in station, ignoble, of low degree, and without the proper pedigree—maybe even those from "the wrong side of the tracks."

"Things which are despised" is rather plain. Hated, abhorred, due every form of abuse and vilification. So, God employs the things that are either low or even lower than that—deemed nonexistent by the world.

The Cross of Christ was and is despised, ridiculed, and scorned to this day.

When Paul preached on Mars Hill he faced a crowd of intellectuals who gathered for public discussion and debate. What the Greeks thought was brilliance, he pointed out, was an ignorant searching for God and His truth. He singled out their inscription TO AN UNKNOWN GOD as an example, declaring that Jesus Christ was the very God which was "unknown" to them, and those Athenians were considered among the most learned men in the world.

In 1 Corinthians 1, Paul also referred to "things which are not" (v. 28). That meant those things or persons which are nonentities to others. They don't rate; they don't fit in; they are ignored. This only amplifies the fact that it is a gross sin to ignore another person—even a derelict or "wino"—because that person is a human being for whom Christ suffered and bled and died. It is a grievous sin to act as though another human being is a nonentity, a nothing. When Jesus declared, "but whosoever shall say, Thou fool, shall be in danger of hell fire," He had in mind this idea of "things which are not." The worst part about the term is not the word "fool" but what it implied—that a person was a dumb, soulless being, and not worthy of even being counted.

You didn't make "Who's Who," but worse than that, you didn't even make "Who's Not"! That's all right. God still has a plan for you.

Yes, God knows exactly what He is doing. He turns the tables. What the world thinks is important may not be so. Wealth, fame, acclaim. None of these are necessary for you to be used of God. So, the people God chooses are, by and large, the plain, simple folks. Now I want to make two things abundantly clear.

1. *He Does Not Say* Not Any Mighty, Not Any Noble.

The passage states "not many" mighty or noble. Thank God for the Ph.D.'s, the entertainers, the athletes, the celebrities who live for God.

Paul was one of the "mighty." Yet, he did not feel he was. He was "a Jew of the Jews," "a Hebrew of the Hebrews," a man of background, breeding, education, and experience. He had all of the credentials. He was also a Roman citizen and even used that to his advantage.

God employed Paul's exceptional gifts for heavenly purposes. But before God could use him, Paul had to be humbled, and his ego had to fall subject unto the Lordship of Christ. To know Christ became to Paul the greatest experience in the world.

> That I may know him, and the power of his resurrection, and the fellowship of his sufferings, being made conformable unto his death (Phil. 3:10).

He concluded that all else but an intimate, personal relationship with Christ was nothing but "dung" (refuse). That point of view had to emerge from Paul's heart and mind before he could be used to the maximum.

God can use extraordinary people only when they are yielded to the matchless Christ. They must lay down all ego and ambition in the dust at His feet.

2. I Am Not Putting a Premium on Laziness or Mediocrity When I Make the Statement That God Uses Ordinary People to His Glory.

You may not have a razor-sharp mind, but you must study. You may not be a genius or a near-genius. You may have scored low on the SAT. You may be puny, may have plain looks. But you must yield all of you to Jesus Christ. That is the crucial point.

Someone has remarked that it does not take much of a person to be a Christian, but it takes all of the person there is. Anything less than your best is not enough. Too long have we preached a watered-down discipleship.

The Lord wants all of you, no matter how imperfect. That is why He commands:

> Thou shalt love the Lord thy God with all thy heart, and with all thy soul, and with all they mind. This is the first and great commandment (Matt. 22:37-38).

If you are not extraordinary, that may simply mean you will have to work harder and study harder than the genius. The old hymn goes, "Every work for Jesus will be blest, But He asks from everyone his best. Our talents may be few, these may be small, But unto Him is due our best, our all." Second Timothy 2:15 implies that we are to be diligent (study) to show ourselves "approved unto God, a workman that needeth not to be ashamed, rightly dividing the word of truth."

You may be a singer with only an ordinary voice, yet it ought to be your ambition to make that voice sing the sweetest notes it can for Jesus. You may not have a strong physique, but every nerve, every fiber, every sinew, and every muscle ought to be dedicated to Jesus Christ.

God never asks us to understand all He is doing. We are merely to accept His "good, and acceptable, and perfect will" (Rom. 12:2*b*).

3. God Uses Ordinary People in Extraordinary Ways.

Christian history is filled with plain men and women who were ordinary but who dedicated their seemingly meager powers to Christ. The early disciples. John Wycliffe, Miles Coverdale, John Tyndale, Clara Barton, John Wesley, D. L. Moody, Fanny J. Crosby. They were either "ordinary" or had severe handicaps.

God absolutely delights in using the ordinary, the handicapped, the wounded. He deliberately chooses plain people to carry out His purposes, and then infuses those people with supernatural power as we shall see.

A woman once explained to Charles Haddon Spurgeon, the great British preacher, "Mr. Spurgeon, I was saved at one time, but now I am lost." Spurgeon replied by asking, "Madam, does God work accidentally or on purpose?"

"On purpose, Sir," she answered.

"Well, Madam, if you were ever saved, you are saved now, for God does everything on purpose—nothing by accident!"

God has chosen you on purpose. God uses plain, ordinary people. And what makes that possible?

GOD'S SPECIAL POWER

> But of him are ye in Christ Jesus, who of God is made unto us wisdom, and righteousness, and sanctification, and redemption (v. 30).

This is exactly how God works. What does this verse teach? That Jesus makes up for our lack. He is our wisdom, our righteousness, our sanctification, and our redemption! This is our position if we have believed: "In Christ Jesus." That is really the only place to be. If I do not have wisdom, He does. Righteousness? He does. His righteousness is imputed to us. It reminds me of that stirring song, "He's Everything to Me."

We may be ordinary, but our God is truly extraordinary.

If only we could learn to let God live His life through us, what a difference it would make. Paul testified, "I am crucified with Christ: nevertheless I live; yet not I, but Christ liveth in me . . ." (Gal. 2:20*a*). We are the temples of the Holy Spirit. The apostle also exulted, "Christ in you, the hope of glory" (Col. 1:27).

After I was already in the ministry, I learned an invaluable lesson. I found out that God did not want me to do anything for Him. Rather, He wanted to do something *through* me. Today many are falling prey to the "New Age" movement. Its followers dote on what they call "channeling." In channeling a guru or teacher from a past existence is supposed to manifest himself through a human channel. The devil always counterfeits what God does.

In the truest sense you and I are channels, conduits of the Lord Jesus Christ. We are His vessels, and He lives in us.

How often I have heard people remark, "Why, I just serve God in my own poor, weak way." Such a statement often belies a mock humility. They want you to brag on them with, "Naw, you're great. It's wonderful what you do for Christ!" If you serve God in your "poor, weak way," quit it!

God wants you to serve Him in *His* dynamic, mighty way, not *your* pitiful, puny way. Let this grip you: "For it is God which worketh in you both to will and to do of his good pleasure" (Phil. 2:13). He works in you if you will let Him. We must reach the place where we cry to Him, "God, I'm tired of being inhibited. I want to be *inhabited* by You. I'm sick of my life as it is, depending on myself and striving to live the Christian life. It's time I let You live your life through me."

Let Him live His life through you, and then you can tell the world, "Nevertheless I live; yet not I, but Christ liveth in me; and the life I now live in the flesh I live by the faith of the Son of God, who loved me, and gave himself for me" (Gal. 2:20).

Coming back to the text, God uses foolish things, weak things, base things, despised things.

When I consider foolish things I think of the late and great evangelist Billy Sunday. Billy was rough-hewn, sometimes rather coarse and crude. When he was converted Sunday was a baseball player with the Chicago White Stockings. When God called him he had no education to speak of. He then became a clerk at the YMCA in Chicago.

He had laughable ideas and used slang language. Many times he would turn flips or do somersaults on the platform. He was known to rip hymn books and break chairs to make a point. Sometimes to illustrate repentance he would do a back flip. He was roundly criticized, yet he was the most successful evangelist of his day. He was the

D. L. Moody, the Billy Graham of his era. Interestingly, Billy Graham's father, Frank Graham, became a Christian in Sunday's 1923 campaign in Charlotte, North Carolina. Who can tell the profound impact Sunday has had on subsequent Christian history? Strange as he was in his methods, it is estimated that over one million were won to Christ during his ministry, a day when there was no sound amplification except a megaphone or a sounding board. Commerical radio came into being only during his last seven years of ministry, and television was nonexistent. To this day I still run into people who were saved as a result of Sunday's ministry. Millions of people will be in heaven either directly or indirectly because of his preaching.

Countless preachers and professors have had all of the accoutrements of learning. They have enough earned degrees to paper the walls of their studies, but many have not been used like a stammering, stuttering D. L. Moody or a crude Billy Sunday. Why does God powerfully use some who appear ill prepared and apparently not use others who have all the credentials and degrees? Could it be that Billy Sunday had tapped a source of power others had neglected? Billy used to lay his sermon notes over Isaiah 61:1 which says "the spirit of the Lord God is upon me because the Lord hath anointed me to preach . . ." Perhaps some others, Dr. Sounding Brass and Professor Tinkling Cymbal, depend upon their learning. I believe God often chooses the "common" person so He can demonstrate His uncanny power to a skeptical world.

God has chosen the weak things. Although the primary meaning of *weak* in this verse relates to physical puniness, it might imply weakness in other areas as well. When I was pastor at Merritt Island, Florida, we had what we called a "Week of Champions." During that week we rented the high school auditorium and had prominent athletes from across the nation present their testimonies. These athletes were affiliated with Athletes in Action and the Fellowship of Christian Athletes.

The following Sunday when I preached, a college student came forward during the invitation. I asked him if and when he was saved. He replied that he had accepted Christ the night Paul Anderson, "the strongest man in the world," was with us. Paul was the Olympic champion weightlifter. He still holds the record for the greatest weight ever lifted—6,270 pounds in a back lift.

I thought to myself, *Boy, that's wonderful! He was won by Paul's testimony*. Paul said the only time he had ever been a ninety-seven pound weakling was when he was four years old. "If the strongest man in the world needs Jesus, so does everyone," he told us. So, I asked that college student, "Well, what was it Paul Anderson said that led you Jesus?" The student said it was nothing that Paul said but it was George Wilson.

Then I remembered George. He was a paraplegic who had been rolled down front in a wheelchair to give his testimony! Men in the audience had lifted the chair, with him in it, onto the platform. With a face shining like Moses' must have when he returned from Mount Sinai, the crippled man had spoken about how the grace and love of the Lord had sustained him.

The college student making the profession of faith continued, "When I saw that crippled man, when I saw his joy, when I saw the reality of the Lord even in his emaciated body, I said to myself, *If God can do that for him, maybe He can do something for me. I* gave my life to Christ. That night the strongest man in the world was bypassed, and God used a paraplegic in a wheelchair to bring that college student to Christ.

God has also chosen the base things of the world. Ignoble. Of low degree. Without standing.

In Judges 6—8 Gideon (Jerubbaal) won a signal victory over the Midianites. When we locate Gideon (6:11) he "threshed wheat by the winepress to hide it from the Midianites." He had kept a low profile. He was afraid the Midianites might pounce on him. On the surface he was a wimp, but God knew better.

"And the angel of the Lord appeared unto him, and said unto him, The Lord is with thee, thou mighty man of valour" (v. 12). Come now, if there was something Gideon was not, it was a man of bravery and courage. At that moment Gideon was a chicken with a capital C. He was hiding out, and yet the angel of the Lord called him a potential hero. And then, to heap abuse on that, the Lord . . .

> . . . looked upon him, and said, Go in this thy might, and thou shalt save Israel from the hand of the Midianites: have not I sent thee? (v. 14).

It is interesting how so many men of God have alibied and shown their inferiority complexes—Abraham, Moses, Elijah, Jeremiah, and Gideon. Gideon argued with God Himself, "How am I going to save Israel? Look, my family is the least in my father's house; we're the poorest in Manasseh!" (see v. 15). In other words, "Of all the tribes Mannaseh is the worst; of all the families in that tribe ours is the poorest; and of all of the kids in my family I am the runt of the litter!" But God must have thought, *Gideon, I can use you!*

You recall the account. God wouldn't let him have an army of 42,000 or 32,000. Gideon ended up with an army of 300! And they routed the army of Midian consisting of 42,000.

Verse 34 of chapter 6 presents an amazing insight from the original language. "But the Spirit of the Lord came upon Gideon . . ." literally means "the Spirit of the Lord clothed Himself with Gideon." God's Spirit moved into Gideon and acted through him. God wore Gideon like we do a suit of clothes. It was no longer Gideon. *It was God in Gideon*. God called an ordinary man and did extraordinary things through him, and God received all the glory.

The Bible also states that God has chosen those things which are despised, those things that are looked down on by others.

Beginning in 1 Samuel 16 we are introduced to David, the son of Jesse. Samuel privately anointed David as Israel's future king. "Now he was ruddy [apple-cheeked] and withal of a beautiful countenance [fair of eyes], and goodly to look to" (v. 12). In chapter 17 David volunteered to fight Goliath, the fearsome giant of the Philistines. David was a kid with peach fuzz on his face . . . up against a monster nine feet tall. Goliath was the "big bad Leroy Brown" of the Philistines. The most experienced Israelite veteran blanched even to hear the giant's voice, much less to glance in his direction. So, little David with the blush of apples on his cheeks, strode out of fight the blasphemous behemoth.

Goliath boomed, "Am I a dog, that thou comest to me with staves?" (1 Sam. 17:43). He yelled, to put it in modern speech, "When I finish with you I am going to feed your pieces to the fowls of the air and the animals of the field!" David answered, "I come to you in the name of the Lord of hosts, the God of Israel, whom you have taunted. This day the Lord will deliver you up into my hands, and I will strike you down and remove your head from you. And I will give the dead bodies of the army of the Philistines this day to the birds of the sky and the wild beasts of the earth, that all the earth may know that there is a God in Israel" (vv. 45*b*-46, NASB).

If Israel had sent out a giant as awesome as Goliath, what would that have proven? Nothing—just a good fight. But when a kid goes out and defeats a giant, people will sit up and take notice. Then people must acknowledge, "There is a God in Israel."

Billy Graham has many times preached that many, many people will be closer to the throne in heaven than he—the unsung, unheralded folks who go about God's business for Him. The minimum-wage clerk, the paper carrier, the physical therapist, the little widow trying to survive by herself, the mission pastor, the missionary seemingly on "the backside of nowhere." And, for a fact, they are really extraordinary. "And those who have insight will shine brightly like the brightness of the expanse of heaven, and those who lead the many to righteousness, like the stars forever and ever" (Dan. 12:3, NASB).

Last of all, recognize . . .

GOD'S SOVEREIGN PURPOSE

Why does God operate like this? In verse 29 of our text is the answer—"that no flesh should glory in his presence." There are not going to be any peacocks in heaven. That's the reason God saves us by His grace. He won't save us by our works, will He? Of course not, because if He did, we could then call ourselves co-saviors. We are saved by grace through faith (see Eph. 2:8-9, Titus 3:5). We can glory in no one but the Lord Jesus Christ.

Further, this is the reason we must continue to give Him the glory. Don't be like the South Georgia woodpecker who was pecking away when a bolt of lightning split his pine tree from top to bottom. Later he was seen with nine other woodpeckers as he proudly pointed out, "There it is, gentlemen, right over there!"

God is not going to judge whether you were rich and famous and highly successful. He will judge you according to whether or not you filled the place He had for you. And what is that place? He is not going to ask whether you were the pastor of a large church, whether you were a best-selling Christian author, whether thousands upon thousands heard you preach. He is going to ask if you were faithful. "Be thou faithful unto death, and I will give thee a crown of life" (Rev. 2:10*d*). What matters is whether you are in the center of His good, and acceptable, and perfect will (see Rom. 12:1-2).

In Christ there is no inferiority. No matter your past feelings of inferiority or inadequacy, you can be an instrument of God. If you want to be, you can be. Sometimes you may not be used of God exactly as you think you should be. That will not matter in God's plan of eternity. If God is in it, you do not choose your place of service. Make yourself available to Him. The greatest ability is availability.

Why not pray, "Lord, inhabit my humanity and do whatever you want to in me. 'Lord, I give myself to Thee, Thine forevermore to be. Lord, I give myself to Thee, Thine forevermore to be.' Lord, make me your instrument"?

6. Banishing the Ghost of Guilt

Love bade me welcome; yet my soul drew back,
Guilty of dust and sin. —George Herbert

Alfred Lord Tennyson, poet laureate of England in a bygone era, wrote this poignant piece entitled "Remorse."

> Shall I kill myself?
> What help in that? I cannot kill
> my sin.
> if soul be soul, nor can I kill my shame;
> No, nor by living can I live it down.
> The days will grow to weeks, the weeks
> to months,
> The months will add themselves and make
> the years,
> The years will roll into centuries,
> And mine shall ever be a name of scorn.

Guilt dogs the footsteps of mankind. Unless a person is totally out of it, and has departed reality, guilt is with him. It gnaws at his vitals, or as one fellow phrased it, "It eats at his innards." Many of us are Lady Macbeths wringing our hands and sobbing, "All the perfumés of Arabia will not sweeten this little hand."

Is there no peace from guilt? Will the ghosts of our guilt always lurk nearby?

John the apostle had rare insight from God into guilt and its implications.

> That which we have seen and heard declare we unto you, that ye also may have fellowship with us: and truly our fellowship is with the Father, and with his Son Jesus Christ. And these things write we unto you, that your joy may be full. This then is the message we have heard of him, and declare unto you, that God is light, and in him is no darkness at all. If we say that we have fellowship with him, and walk in darkness, we lie, and do not the truth. But if we walk in the light as he is in the light, we have fellowship one with another, and the blood of Jesus Christ his Son cleanseth us from all sin. If we say that we have no sin, we deceive ourselves, and the truth is not in us. If we confess our sins he is faithful and just to forgive us our sins and to cleanse us from all unrighteousness. If we say that we have not sinned, we make him a liar, and his word is not in us (1 John 1:3-10).

All of these verses present basically the same truth—the enemy of joy is the breaking of fellowship with God. And the cause of the breaking of fellowship is sin. Sin separates us from God. Sin also severs our fellowship with brothers and sisters in Christ. This chapter deals with the sins of the saints.

First, I want you to notice what I call . . .

THE CONCEALING OF SIN IN THE LIFE OF THE CHRISTIAN

The first impulse of the average Christian when he sins is to cover it up. "To err is human." To cover it up is, also.

Verse 5 makes it plain: "God is light, and in Him there is no darkness at all." Light stands for clarity and *purity*. You can collect the grungiest, filthiest garbage and shine a light on it. The light may reveal that rotten mess, but that garbage will never contaminate the light. The light is as pure as it ever was.

Light not only speaks of the purity of our Lord but also His *power*. Light is invincible. The enemy of light is darkness, and darkness has no power against light.

But light also implies *productivity*. In grammar school you no doubt learned about the process of photosynthesis. Plants contain chlorophyll. When the light shines on the plant, that process begins to work. The plant grows and grows, becomes more productive, gives off oxygen for animals to breathe, and takes in carbon dioxide which animals and man give off. We eat the animals and the plants, and life is sustained. Where does that immense energy come from? From the light of the sun. We live in a world that is sustained by light.

Life and light are linked together. "In him [Jesus] was life; and the life was the light of men. And the light shineth in darkness; and the darkness comprehended it not" (John 1:4-5). John in his Gospel and in his Epistles was caught up in Jesus as the Life and the Light and the embodiment of Love. Light is desirable and pleasant.

One of the punishments of hell is it is a place of outer darkness. Hell is also a place of fire, but it must not give off light, for hell is described as an abode of darkness. As far as I can ascertain, not one glimmer, not one glow, not one beam, not one ray of light will ever shine upon the unsaved in eternity. Eternal, outer darkness. But in heaven there will be no need for sun by day or moon by night, for Jesus, the Lamb, will be the light of that eternal city.

Notice the *light* but, in contrast, also the *lie* in verse 6. "If we say we have fellowship with him, and walk in darkness, we lie, and do not the truth."

That is plain enough. The person who claims he is in fellowship with God, and yet walks in darkness, is a liar. The Bible asks, "What fellowship hath light with darkness?" If you put light with darkness, the darkness will soon be gone. Light dispels and drives away darkness.

"I wandered in the shades of night 'til Jesus came to me, and with the sunlight of His smile bade all my darkness flee."

Now focus on the evolution of a lie. There is a phrase which shows up four times here:

Verse 6..."If we say . . ."

Verse 8..."If we say . . ."

Verse 10..."If we say . . ."

Chapter 2, verse 4..."He that sayeth . . ."

We may claim, we may say, but what we do is what counts. Sin begins kind of small, we think, and then it grows like a noxious weed.

Right off the bat, when a person has sin in his life, he starts to cover up. He even begins to exaggerate and prevaricate to others about his sins. Watergate. The Iran-Contra Hearings. The Teapot Dome Scandal years ago. Those were minor in comparison to what many others have done about lying in reference to their sins.

Verse 6 goes: "If we say that we have fellowship with him, and walk in darkness, we lie and do not the truth." When a person has more and more sin creeping into his life, he will cover up. He acts like he has fellowship with God, and he may keep on coming to church.

He puts on a facade. He acts as though nothing has happened. First, a fellow lies to others about his sins. He puts on a false face, a front.

But what else happens? He begins to lie to himself. That is deadly serious. Verse 8: "If we say that we have no sin, we *deceive ourselves*, and the truth is not in us." What a deception—believing one's own lies. A person can try to live in a fantasy world long enough until he will actually have difficulty separating the fact from the fantasy. Many a Christian who was dedicated and devoted to the Lord has gradually drifted into a life-style that is totally incompatible with the Christian walk. And he begins to think to himself, *Well, it must be all right. Just about everybody's doing that except a few old fuddy duddies*.

He becomes a double-minded man. His spirit chides, "You've sinned." But his mind says, "No, I haven't." So, he becomes unstable, a spiritual schizophrenic. He is mentally and morally unbalanced, actually mentally sick. James says "a double-minded [souled] man is unstable in all his ways" (Jas. 1:8).

It is tragic, but many Christians are, like the popular song, "Telling lies, sweet little lies." Only their lies bear bitter fruit. They have never reached the point where they have spiritual maturity, where their body is full of light and their eye is single.

We begin to lie to others. Then we even begin to lie to ourselves.

Worst of all, we begin to lie to God. Verse 10 goes: "If we say that we have not sinned, we make him [God] a liar, and his truth is not in us." We have no method of estimating how many Christians lie in all three areas. If most of us are honest, we will have to confess that at one time or another, we have lied to all three. How can we possibly try lying to the Holy Spirit? Ananias tried it. That is dangerous business. "Oh, no, Lord, I haven't sinned. That was just a mixup. That was a slip of the tongue. It was a mistake. It was a glandular malfunction—but, Lord, it wasn't sin."

We try to deny it by renaming it or explaining it away. "Lord, my wife doesn't understand me." "God, my husband is so brutal and insensitive." "My parents don't give me enough allowance, so I just took that money. Lord, I needed it."

The Holy Spirit works on us. The message is conveyed that we have sinned. God declares, "You have sinned." You reply, "No way. I haven't sinned." Who's lying? If we say we have no sin, we deceive ourselves.

The person who goes through all these machinations to cover up for his sins—past, present, and future—is woefully out of fellowship with God.

That person simply does not have joy in his life. We have seen the *Light,* God. We have looked at the *lie*. Now there is the *loss,* the loss of fellowship. When you have sin in your life, and you will not deal with it, you will have a miserable existence. Life will drag like a giant tortoise from day to day. When you try to pray it will feel as though the heavens are composed of brass. You will have no peace, no power, no productivity, no seeming potential. Verse 4 goes: "These things write we unto you, that your joy may be full." There is only one factor that can snatch away your joy—sin. That is it. Only one kind of sin—yours.

"It's not my brother, not my sister, but it's me, O Lord, standing in the need of prayer." This is personal. Your sin will chase the joy out of your life. Yet, the worst aspect of the Christian's sin is not only what it does to him but what it does to his Savior. Charles Haddon Spurgeon wrote: "The sins of the ungodly plunge the spear into Jesus' side. The sins of the Christian plunge it into His heart."

There is the loss of *fellowship*. There is the loss of *joy*. The most miserable person on the face of the earth is not a lost man but rather he is a saved man out of fellowship with God. His entire being suffers, his body, his mind, his soul, his spirit. From the top of his head to the soles of his feet. Hurt. Pain. Remorse. Confusion. Anxiety. The Christian out of fellowship is like a bone out of joint, an abscessed tooth, broken bones that are not set. The backslidden Christian is a miserable monstrosity. Yet, on the other hand, many unsaved people are having a ball. There is no point approaching an unsaved person with, "Hey, man, you can't have any fun if you're not saved." The Bible speaks of the pleasures of sin, but they are only for a season.

"The bread of deceit is sweet, but afterward a man's mouth shall be filled with gravel;" (Prov. 20:17). There is a certain amount of sensual pleasure in sin. The devil is too smart to go fishing without bait on his hook. In this life, a lost man may not be as miserable as a saved person who is double-minded because there is sin in his life, and he is unstable in all his ways. Billy Graham used to refer to the double-minded man as a person "with one foot in the world and one foot in the church."

So, there is the *Light*. God is the Light. Then there is the *lie*. We say we have no sin or either, like certain people, we say we have not sinned. Regardless, those assumptions are outright lies. All of these refer to *the concealing of sin in the life of a Christian* and lead to terrible loss.

Second of all, I want us to examine . . .

THE REVEALING OF SIN IN THE LIFE OF THE CHRISTIAN

What does light do? It reveals, and that is needed. It has been said that a clear conscience is frequently the result of a poor memory.

In verse 5 our text states that God is light. God shines His light upon our sins to reveal them.

You will never become a victorious Christian unless you experientially know these principles of how God convicts of sin. Many cannot ascertain between Holy Spirit conviction and Satanic accusation. The Holy Spirit convicts us of sin, while the devil accuses us of sin.

The devil is like the prosecuting attorney. He is constantly pointing the finger of accusation at us. Satan is an adversary (Num. 22:22; 2 Sam. 19:22; 1 Kings 5:4,11:25). In Job (1:6*ff.*, 2:1*ff.*) he is seen as an accuser. Throughout the Bible he is revealed as a liar, a murderer, a recognized accuser (Matt. 4:1,10), and in other nefarious roles. He is accusing you before God and before yourself. He is the accuser of the brethren.

But the Holy Spirit is not an accuser. He is the Convictor. And you are not going to have genuine peace and joy until you learn the difference between Satanic accusation and Holy Spirit conviction.

> And when he [the Holy Spirit] is come, he will reprove [convict] the world of sin, and of righteousness, and of judgment: Of sin because they believe not on me; Of righteousness because I go to my Father, and ye see me no more; Of judgment, because the prince of this world [Satan, the devil] is judged (John 16:8-11).

What will happen when the Holy Spirit convicts you of your sins? In the first place, God is going to convict you of sin *legitimately*. That is, the Holy Spirit will never convict you of a sin that has already been cleansed.

First John 1:7 ought to be one of your favorite verses: "the blood of Jesus Christ, God's Son, cleanseth us from all sin." God will never bring up again any sin that He has placed under the blood. This truth was revealed to Peter on the rooftop at Joppa when the sheet was let down with all kinds of "unclean," unkosher things in it. After Peter protested God's request to "kill, and eat," God told him, "What God hath cleansed, that call not thou common" [or unclean] (Acts 10:13,15).

What happens when God cleanses me of my sin? *He forgets it.* "For I will forgive their iniquities, and their sin I will remember no more" (Jer. 31:34, NASB). The Bible asserts that confessed and forgiven sin is cast behind God's back, is buried in the depths of the sea, is removed as far as the east is from the west—so far has He removed our transgressions from us. "Gone, gone, gone, gone. Yes, my sins are gone."

God would not be just if those cleansed sins were called back before you. If you have confessed and you have turned those sins over to Jesus, and you have forsaken those sins, yet they keep coming up in your mind, it is the devil who is accusing you, not the Holy Spirit. You ought to repudiate the devil. Call him the liar he is. God will not demand double jeopardy. He will not summon you before the court a second time to answer for a sin He has already remitted.

The Holy Spirit will convict you not only *legitimately* but also *specifically*. Verse 9 has it: "If we confess our sins." Plural—not our *sin,* not the sin nature, but our sins. S-I-N-S. The Holy Spirit will not leave you hanging in the air. He will convict you of those specific sins. Miss Bertha Smith rightly teaches that we are to confess our sins "up to date." If we do, there will be no question concerning the source of irritation and vexation. It is coming from self or Satan, but not from God.

In Holy Spirit conviction He will spell out those unconfessed, uncleansed sins. "You were greedy." "You were haughty." "You lost your temper." You were unkind." "You had lustful thoughts." "You failed to witness when you could have." The Holy Spirit will name those sins one by one. On the other hand, the devil is devious as usual. If it is a specific sin, he will never bring it up until God has already forgiven and cleansed you. He never accuses you specifically. He does it generally, so you will have a vague, uneasy feeling about your general spiritual condition. He wants you to feel absolutely miserable about nothing in particular. If he can sidetrack you, he will have achieved his purpose. He wants you to have this constant emotionally drained, tired, rundown feeling which weighs heavily on you. He will whisper deep down inside, "You are no good. You are a sinner. You are unworthy. You don't deserve to live. God is not going to hear you. God doesn't love you. You're a vile sinner. And you ought to feel bad!"

That is not the Holy Spirit speaking to you. The Spirit is personal and pointed. His conviction is pertinent. He names your sins so He can deal with them. On the opposite pole, the devil wants you to feel rejected and not accepted, even though you are already "accepted in the beloved."

We are already royal bluebloods. We are children of the King. The devil hates our position in Christ. So, since he cannot have us, he wants to make us so miserable and nonproductive that we are pathetic cases.

A huge percentage of Christians spend so much time on their maintenance that they do not have a moment to be concerned about others. They dissect themselves piece by piece and then put themselves back together. They become their own psychologists, and they read books and listen to tapes—and that is OK if it is godly material—and all too often end up being analyzed by psychologists and psychiatrists who sometimes are not Christians. I call their pursuit morbid introspection.

It is not essential for you to do that. It is kind of like do-it-yourself brain surgery. It will not work. Rather, you need to pray, "Search me, O God, and know my heart: try me, and know my thoughts" (Ps. 139:23). Then read the following verse: "And see if there be any wicked way in me, and lead me in the way everlasting" (v. 24).

How could one's deceitful heart diagnose that same deceitful heart?

It is impossible. It would be like President Nixon investigating Watergate. But the Holy Spirit of God can do it. He will convict you of sin. Then, when He names it, you confess it. If He does not call it to mind, never mind it! The Spirit will convict you *legitimately* and *specifically*. We receive forgiveness by naming what He names and confessing it. Count your many sins and name them one by one. Call them by name, and through the Spirit get rid of them.

And then the Spirit convicts you *redemptively*. The devil accuses you to make you despair, to push you away from Christ. The devil wants you bowed beneath a load of guilt to the point you are driven to the brink. The devil accuses you to destroy you. Of course, he may not destroy you physically, but he can work on you until you are a physical, emotional, and mental wreck. Do not let the accuser of the brethren grind you into the ground and force you into despair.

The Holy Spirit convicts you to *reclaim* you. Why did John write his first Epistle? "That your joy might be full." The Spirit is not trying to punish us. He is trying to correct us and to usher us back into full fellowship with the Lord, so we might have joy. He draws us to Christ so we can confess our sins and be cleansed.

First, we have seen *the concealing of sin in the life of a Christian;* second, *the revealing of sin in the life of a Christian,* and how the Holy Spirit does that. Finally let us look at . . .

THE DEALING WITH SIN IN THE LIFE OF THE CHRISTIAN

How do we deal with sin? What is the remedy once we have seen the problem in our own hearts? Once the Holy Spirit has impressed us with, "This is where you are wrong," what do we do?

To the sinning Christian this verse ought to be heavenly music: "If we confess our sins, he is faithful and just to forgive us our sins, and to cleanse us from all unrightousness." First, we deal with sin by *confession*. Understand what the word *confession* means, for it is technical. It does not merely mean to admit your sin. Many people have admitted their sins but have never truly confessed them. Often I have heard people remark: "Yeah, I've sinned. All have sinned. Sure, we're sinners." That is not confession. That is merely admission.

In the original language "confess" was a cognate of two words, meaning "to say the same as" or "to agree." It means not only to admit but also to agree with—with God, of course, and what He knows about your sins.

Many Christians have misunderstood 1 John 1:9. They have thought, *Hey, that's all I have to do. "Lord, I did it. Now You forgive me."* But it means more than that. It means that I agree and concur with what God says about my sins. It means to agree with Him all up and down the line.

God says, "That is a sin." We say, "Yes, Lord, I agree. It is a sin."

God says, "That is wrong." We say, "Yes, Lord, it is wrong."

God says, "You need to repent of that bad temper." You say, "Yes, I do need to get that right."

All of us could compile individual lists of sins. It is still not enough to agree with the fact that this or that is a sin. God may say, "You ought not to have that in your life." You agree with Him. And here comes the hard part. God says, "You ought to give it up." God then says, "You will, won't you?" You answer, "Yes, Lord, I give it up right now." I agree with God and come over and line up against my sin or sins, not merely admit them.

You will never be done with that sin until you, in your own heart, judge it to be wrong, taking sides against that sin. The way to deal with your sins is to say what God says about them.

Not only must you confess that sin, but you must deal with it by *confidence*.

John writes further:

> My little children, these things write I unto you, that ye sin not. And if any man sin, we have an *advocate* with the Father, Jesus Christ the righteous. And he is the propitiation for our sins: and not for ours only, but also for the sins of the whole world (1 John 2:1-2).

"Advocate" means that Jesus Christ is our defense lawyer, and He has never lost a case for one of His born-again clients. Remember that Satan is the prosecuting attorney. Pause right here. How do I know my sins are going to be forgiven if I confess them? How can I be sure? Because of my Lawyer.

That is what Paul had in mind when he wrote, "Who shall lay any thing to the charge of God's elect? It is God that justifieth" (Rom. 8:33). In other words, sinners may try to bring charges against you. The devil himself will try, but it is not going to work.

First John 2:2 bears repeating: "And he is the propitiation for our sins . . ." Propitiation means the substitutionary sacrifice. Jesus satisfied all the demands of the law. He paid the price for our redemption. Because He died He is the satisfaction for my sin.

He is our lawyer, and what He does is to plead His blood. His blood is the finished work. His intercession is the unfinished work. He will stand in for you and defend your case until He returns for you and me. He died for you and me, and our sins have been paid for. Praise God, I can confess my sin and deal with my guilt.

Confession and confidence lead to cleansing. It is cleansing that we need. Psychology always deals with guilt feelings but never guilt. No psychologist or psychiatrist can ever take away an ounce of guilt. All they can do is deaden the feeling, rationalize, or explain.

But, thank God, "the blood of Jesus Christ his Son cleanseth us from all sin" (1 John 1:7).

> There is a fountain filled with blood
> Drawn from Immanuel's veins;
> And sinners plunged beneath that flood,
> Lose all their guilty stains,
> Lose all their guilty stains,
> Lose all their guilty stains;
> And sinners, plunged beneath that flood,
> Lose all their guilty stains.
>
> —William Cowper

7. What a Friend

In Him I found a house, a bed,
A table, company. —Roger Williams

Thomas Wolfe, the genius-author best known for his novel *You Can't Go Home Again,* once wrote about loneliness:

> Loneliness, far from being a rare and curious phenomenon . . . is the central and inevitable fact of human existence. When we examine the moments, acts, and statements of all kinds of people—not only the grief and ecstasy of the greatest poets, but also the huge unhappiness of the average soul, as evidenced by the innumerable strident words of abuse, hatred, contempt, mistrust and scorn that forever grate upon our ears as the manswarm passes us in the streets—we find, I think, that they are all suffering from the same thing. The final cause of their complaint is loneliness.[1]

The late and great Christian psychiatrist from Switzerland, Dr. Paul Tournier, wrote that loneliness is the most devastating malady of this age. Loneliness is not a curious abstraction, not a far-out notion. It is common throughout the human race. It will strike all of us at one time or another.

Literature and music are laden with the theme of loneliness. People the world over are overwhelmed with loneliness. "Only the Lonely," "None But the Lonely Heart," "Alone Again, Naturally; "I'm So Lonesome I Could Die," "Lonely Girl," and "All by Myself" are typical song titles.

God pity all the lonely Folk
With Griefs they do not tell
Women waking in the night
And men dissembling well.
—Louise Driscoll

When I remember all the friends
so link'd together
I've seen around me fall
Like leaves in wintry weather
I feel like one
Who treads alone
Some banquet hall deserted, . . .
—Thomas Moore

In *The Human Comedy,* Homer's loving, wise mother counseled him, "The loneliness you feel has come to you because you are no longer a child. But the whole world has always been full of that loneliness. The loneliness does not come from the war. The war did not make it. It was the loneliness that made the war. It was the despair in all things for no longer having the grace of God."[2]

People, for the most part, do not want to live alone. Neither do they want to die alone.

The Psalmist sang of his loneliness and feelings of estrangement and isolation.

> I am like a pelican of the wilderness: I am like an owl of the desert. I watch, and am as a sparrow alone upon the house top (Ps. 102:6-7).

Loneliness had swept over the psalmist's heart, mind, soul, and spirit. If a sparrow could reason and think as a human being, and he did not realize that God cares for him, how insignificant he would feel. So teeny and tiny, so frail and weak, but the Omnipotent God conducts a funeral for the little bird when he dies. There is an isolated owl of the desert, but who gives a hoot? Out there is a pelican in a swampy wilderness.

Do not think it is only the widow all by herself who is lonely. People from every station and walk of life experience loneliness—the high and low, the rich and poor, the young and old.

Think about the rich and famous who died in loneliness within the last twenty-five or thirty years. Marilyn Monroe, who had the world at her feet, died from an overdose of sleeping pills. Janis Joplin, queen of the rock singers in the Sixties, OD'd from heroin in her Los Angeles apartment. Shortly before she died she confessed to an acquaintance, "After I come off the stage, all I do is sit around and watch TV, and I am so very lonely."

One comedian was so lonely he would hire people to sit up with him all night long because he was afraid to go to sleep by himself. Thousands of mates are left alone each year as their marriages are severed by death, separation, or divorce.

H. G. Wells, the noted British scientist-historian-lecturer-author, is considered by many the greatest intellect of the twentieth century. Before he died he plainly stated, "I am lonely."

What is loneliness? *People often confuse solitude with loneliness*. A certain amount of solitude is essential. From time to time we must withdraw to "collect our wits," to meditate, to pray, to commune with God.

> We all have a need for solitude. I think there may be as many people suffering from the lack of solitude as there are those suffering from too much. I certainly felt this the sixteen years we lived in Japan. I am sure it is hard for people who have never been there to imagine the crowded conditions. If you can imagine half of the population of the United States crowded into a land smaller than the state of California you will get an idea of the crowds. It is no wonder that more of the Japanese work at this business of developing inner solitude than we do in the United States.
>
> The great potential in the human soul has often been manifested in those who sought creative and recreative solitude. Jesus Christ stayed in seclusion for thirty years before coming forth to spend His three years among the crowds. Even so, we are constantly reminded, as in Matthew 14:23, of His turning aside to be alone and to pray: "And when he had sent the multitudes away, he went up into a mountain

> apart to pray: and when the evening was come, he was there alone." This was the pattern of His life. He went aside to meditate and to remember that He and the Father were One, and that He was there to do the Father's will.[3]

You can be alone and not lonely. If you are one of those people who can never be alone, or you panic, you have a problem. Jesus left us an example by ministering and being in the midst of crowds—that was essential to His calling—but then He withdrew to be alone with the Father and the Holy Spirit. Some people may not want to be alone because they cannot stand themselves. They do not want to look themselves or God in the face.

There is also a difference between being lonesome and lonely. You can be lonesome when you are away from home, family, and friends. It happens to those who travel. Many consultants, salesmen, truck drivers, and others are away from home 200 to 250 nights a year.

Years ago there was a book and a play entitled *The Face in the Crowd. And you can be lonely in a crowd.* In fact, sometimes the loneliness can be worse amid hundreds or thousands of people. Henry David Thoreau commented that a city is a place where hundreds of people are alone together.

Lonely people at times look at others in a public place, and they feel even worse about their loneliness. All around them are seemingly happy people, laughing, chatting, having fun. No wonder there are "lonely hearts" clubs and all kinds of bars and night clubs. Of course, many lonely people are not looking in the right places for interaction with other human beings. Drive past those places on any night of the week, and many of them are jampacked. Lonely people are often there until the doors are closed, even though they have to be at work only a few hours later. People are lonely, and they want someone to recognize them as human beings.

They feel like a pelican in the wilderness, an owl in the desert, a sparrow on a rooftop. I remember that song we used to sing as kids:

"Here I sit like a bird in the wilderness, bird in the wilderness, bird in the wilderness."

Loneliness is not lonesomeness. It is not isolation. It is insulation, feeling cut off, unnoticed, unloved, uncared for, unneeded, maybe even unnecessary.

Every one of us has three basic psychological and spiritual needs. One, *every person needs someone to love and with whom to share intimately*. Two, *we all need someone who understands us and knows how we feel, someone who says, "I understand, and I care*. Third, *we need to be needed and wanted*. If you are lacking in these areas, you are definitely lonely.

THE CAUSES OF LONELINESS

Why is loneliness such *a common fact?*

1. *A feeling of rejection that many suffer*

Many lonely people have tried and tried again to make and keep friends, but they have suffered rejection, real or imagined. Sometimes the rejection is through no fault of their own. They have been burned in a love relationship or gone through a painful divorce. Perhaps they have been spurned, ignored, put down. As a result their emotions are burnt out. They feel depression but also an emotional deadness and numbness. Many a love song has echoed these sentiments. "I'll never fall in love again." "There goes my everything." "Cry."

"All the lonely people" walk around with a hurt somewhere. They have an unhealed inner wound and a feeling of futility. They are afraid to try again. They are scared to make themselves vulnerable—and to develop a deep friendship or love relationship, vulnerability must come about.

2. *A basic sense of insecurity*

Some seem to have no self-worth. They do not view themselves as worthy of having even one friend. Because of fear they build a wall between themselves and others. They may operate in society, go to work, and relate to a few people out of sheer necessity, but they act as if they want nothing to do with others if they can help it. They have never accepted themselves, and they think that anyone who would is nutty. Those who cannot accept themselves cannot really accept others. Rather than building bridges, they continue to brick themselves in. Anyone who tries to reach them is "suspect."

3. *A loss of perspective because of sorrow or tragedy*

Many are lonely because they have gone through sorrow, tragedy, or a deep loss. They feel that no one sincerely cares and understands. Nothing really seems to make sense to them. They have lost their sense of perspective, and all of life is tinctured by the pain of their loss.

From a human standpoint Job had lost everything but a bitter wife, his "comforters," and his everpresent, "Why?" People who have a fuzzy perspective because of grief and sorrow have a kinship with Job.

His lament expresses the negative, pessimistic side of life:

> He hath put my brethren far from me, and mine acquaintance are verily estranged from me. My kinsfolk have failed, and my familiar friends have forgotten me. They that dwell in mine house, and my maids, count me for a stranger: I am an alien in their sight. I called my servant, and he gave me no answer; I intreated him with my mouth. My breath is strange to my wife, though I intreated for the children's sake of mine own body. Yea, young children despised me; I arose, and they spake against me. And my inward friends abhorred me: and they whom I loved are turned against me (Job 19:13-19).

Was it all that bad? At the moment it was to Job. Like many who have lost a clear outlook on life, he blamed God. "Know now that God hath overthrown me, and hath compassed me with his net . . . He hath fenced up my way that I cannot pass, and he hath set darkness in my paths. He hath stripped me of my glory, and taken the crown from my head" (19:6,8-9). God had not done that to Job—God had allowed Satan to assail Job for a season.

How often I have heard folks groan, "It's no use. Life is not worth living. There's nothing left. No one cares, and I am all alone." Job had turned inward and had erected a prism of icicles around his soul.

As you realize, Job came through with the help of his best friend, the Lord. "So the Lord blessed the latter end of Job more than his beginning" (Job 42:12).

4. *Selfishness*

You cannot control most of the sorrow which benumbs you, but you do have power over selfish attitudes and impulses. Face it. Certain people are lonely because of their own fault. They are self-centered and wrapped up in their own lives. They make it clear that the world revolves around them. In conversation it is a monologue of "I" this and "I" that. If you try to love a selfish person, or do love him, all the two of you will have in common is your mutual love for him.

The selfish person does want friends but ends up having few, if any. Since the selfish one makes a little demigod out of himself, he certainly desires a circle of admirers who will feed his ego and, yes, worship him. The late British philosopher Bertrand Russell noted, "Every man would like to be God if it were possible; some few find it difficult to admit the impossibility."

Jack Hyles has said: "There is no life so empty as a self-centered life, and no life so centered and full as a self-emptied life." There is the difference between the servant of self and the servant of the Savior.

Self-centeredness—selfishness, self-will, rebellion, unbelief—were at the core of the fall in the Garden of Eden. Satan's pitch to Eve was: "Ye shall be as gods, knowing good and evil" (Gen. 3:5).

5. *Depersonalization*

Depersonalization also adds to loneliness. At the airport computerized, robot-like voices direct you: "You are now entering Module A. Move away from the door." (How did he or it know I was standing near the door?) Climb in these new cars, and they talk to you, sometimes in a Japanese accent, "You're running out of gas." It's enough to have a wife instructing you without the dashboard joining in! Enter the average department store, and you can often make a transaction, credit card and all, without ever having eye contact with the salesperson. We are a piece of plastic and a number.

But thank God for Jesus Christ, our *personal* Savior, who gives us a name rather than a number. Personalization is God's approach to us. Depersonalization seems to be the trend of our time. Someone has said, "The more machines act like men, the more men will act like machines." Prophecy teaches that the coming Antichrist will turn the world into a vast concentration camp, with all the inmates numbered.

But Jesus knows His sheep by name: "I am the good shepherd, and know my sheep, and am known of mine" (John 10:14). Stuart Hamblin, after receiving Christ as personal Savior, wrote: "There is no night, for in His light, You'll never walk alone, Always feel at home, Wherever you may roam."

Yet, for most people loneliness is a *common fact*. It is also . . .

A CRIPPLING FORCE

Not long ago they surveyed a large number of patients who had undergone heart attacks. It was found that 50 percent of them were feeling depressed and lonely when their attacks occurred. It was estimated that 80 percent of those who sought psychiatric help came primarily because of feelings associated with loneliness.

Those who counsel people with suicidal tendencies discover feelings of loneliness, along with estrangement. There is self-pity with the expressed or unexpressed emotion of "Nobody cares" and "Nothing matters anymore."

Oftentimes loneliness, or feelings of loneliness, cause anorexia or bulimia or, on the other hand, compulsive eating. Drug use, alcoholism. Insomnia or, conversely, oversleeping.

> A person who wallows in loneliness, who doesn't adapt to an "alone" situation, usually shows signs of self-pity. Resentment, cynicism, sarcasm, and social fear often set in. The person sometimes finds himself daydreaming and withdrawing. There's no logic to it. Loneliness trig-

> gered by the state of aloneness makes the person want to be more alone. Somehow prolonged loneliness fails to reveal any productive elements. Indeed, this emotion actually makes a person unproductive . . . It hardly seems that it is God's design to live with prolonged loneliness.[4]

A CERTAIN CURE

Your loneliness does not have to eat you alive, does not have to consume you, does not have to destroy you. After all is said and done, the answer to loneliness is Jesus. Why? Jesus understands your loneliness.

Psalm 102:6-7, which I quoted earlier, is a Messianic psalm, a prophecy of Jesus Himself, the coming King, God's Anointed One. Those feelings of isolation and loneliness were experienced by our Lord Jesus.

Isaiah foretold the agony of the Messiah in the psalm of the Suffering Servant, chapter 53.

> He is despised and rejected of men; a man of sorrows, and acquainted with grief: and we hid our faces from him; he was despised, and we esteemed him not (v. 3).

John reported that "He came unto his own, and his own received him not" (1:11). In many respects He lived a life of loneliness. For a time Mary His mother and His half brothers did not understand Him. Neither did His disciples. "The foxes have holes, and the birds of the air have nests;" said Jesus, "but the Son of man hath not where to lay his head" (Matt. 8:20). When the multitudes finally began to understand the requirements of following Him, they "bailed out." "And he said, Therefore said I unto you, that no man can come unto me, except it were given unto him of my Father. From that time many of his disciples went back, and walked no more with him. Then said Jesus unto the twelve, Will ye also go away?" (John 6:65-67).

His life and ministry were filled with misunderstandings by others, false accusations against His character and background, insults on his person, chicanery against him, threats of death, persecution, trumped-up charges by the religious leaders, torture and abuse, and finally a horrendous death in the company of two criminals.

As He died on the Cross He cried, "My God, My God, why hast thou forsaken Me?" Messianic Psalm 22 begins with those exact words—the cry of the lonely Savior. As He carried the weight of the world's sin upon Him, God the Father in holiness and righteousness turned away from Him. No one has ever been as lonely as Jesus was at that moment. He was cut off from earth and heaven.

When King David was dying he could sing, "Yea, though I walk through the valley of the shadow of death, I will fear no evil, for Thou art with me," but Jesus had to walk that lonesome valley all by Himself. He died alone.

> My Father's house of light,
> My glory-circled throne,
> I left for earthly night,
> For wand'rings sad and lone
>
> —Frances Ridley Havergal

What does all of this mean to you and me? It demonstrates emphatically that Jesus knows how we feel. He does care and understand, even though no one else may. Hebrews 4:15 comforts us: "For we have not an high priest which cannot be touched with the feeling of our infirmities; but was in all points tempted like as we are, yet without sin." "Jesus knows the pain we feel, He can save and He can heal. Take your burden to the Lord and leave it there."

I remind you that loneliness in itself is not a sin. It may be cultivated by your sin, and you may allow it to dominate your emotions to the exclusion of all else.

When you are lonely, think of Jesus as being lonely and isolated. Jesus alone can meet those three basic needs—someone to love, someone who understands, the need to be needed and wanted. You may reply, "But I need somebody real." That is part of your problem.

Jesus is real. If you have received Him, He lives in you. He is closer to you than anyone else can be.

"But I need somebody here now." He is here now if you have invited Him in. He has promised never to leave you or forsake you. David called Him "a friend that sticketh closer than a brother." Jesus is your friend. Others have disappointed you and broken your heart, but He never will.

> Henceforth I call you not servants; for the servant knoweth not what his lord doeth: but I have called you friends; for all things that I have heard of my Father I have made known unto you (John 15:15).

What a friend we have in Jesus!

I go for a drive with Jesus. We take a walk. We talk together. "Jesus loves me, this I know." And I love Him in return. "And He walks with me, and He talks with me, and He tells me I am His own." I can share anything with him, no matter how intimate or silly or far-fetched—and He will understand. He knows when I'm up and when I'm down. He told you (Matt. 10:30) that "the very hairs of your head are all numbered." Is that closeness? Is that nearness? Is that keeping up with us? Jokingly, more than one bald-headed man has asked, "Where do I fit in?" The answer: "He numbers the pores of their skin and their hair follicles!" He has all of the bases covered, and He leaves nothing undone. And the apostle Peter urged you to cast "all your care upon him; for he careth for you" (1 Pet. 5:7).

Surprisingly, he needs you. That is another reason you do not have to feel lonely and unneeded. The Bible is replete with people Jesus needed and wanted. I think of Zacchaeus, the lonely, hated, isolated tax collector at Jericho. You remember his climb into the sycamore tree. Jesus came along, looked at him in the tree, called him by his right name, and invited Himself to lunch with the Zacchaeus family. I sort of believe Zacchaeus thought to himself, *How do you like that. Jesus knows me! He wants me. He needs me. Isn't that something?*

Believe this: Jesus would have died for you if you had been the only person ever to live on planet Earth. The Model Prayer, often called The Lord's Prayer, begins: "Our Father which art in heaven, hallowed be thy name." A little girl misquoted it innocently, "Our Father which art in heaven, how does He know my name?" Yes, the very God of the universe knows your name and your frame. You are so significant to Him that He died for you.

Not only does He understand how you feel and not only does He meet your need for a friend, but He is always there. You may be alone, but with Him you never have to be lonely.

> For I am persuaded, that neither death, nor life, nor angels, nor principalities, nor powers, nor things present, nor things to come, Nor height, nor depth, nor any other creature, shall be able to separate us from the love of God, which is in Christ Jesus our Lord (Rom. 8:38-39).

We will never be separated from Him. Not even the devil and the denizens of hell can break up our relationship with Christ. David reinforced this truth when he sang: "When my father and mother forsake me, then the Lord will take me up" (Ps. 27:10).

You may have seasons of loneliness, but that feeling does not have to master you. Because Jesus is with you, you need never to be really lonely. We ought to resurrect that old hymn:

> I've seen the lightning flashing,
> I've heard the thunder roll,
> I've felt sin's breakers dashing,
> Trying to conquer my soul.
> I've heard the voice of Jesus,
> Telling me still to fight on,
> He promised never to leave me,
> Never to leave me alone.
>
> No, never alone. No, never alone.
> He promised never to leave me,
> Never to leave me alone,
> No, never alone. No, never alone.

He promised never to leave me,
Never to leave me alone.
—Author Unknown

NOTES

1. Thomas Wolfe, *The Hills Beyond* (New York: Harper Brothers, 1941), p. 186.
2. William Saroyan, *The Human Comedy* ((New York: Harcourt, Brace & Co., 1944), pp. 34-35.
3. Ida Nelle Hollaway, *Loneliness: The Untapped Resource* (Nashville: Broadman Press, 1982), pp. 76-77.
4. Ralph Speas, *How to Deal with How You Feel* (Nashville: Broadman Press, 1980), p. 91.

8. Say No to Fear

Courage is fear
That has said its prayers. —Karle Wilson Baker

Ann Landers, who has written an advice column for over three decades, reports that she receives over 10,000 letters a week, with more mail concerning one particular difficulty than any other.

Is it sex? No. Children? No. Finances? No. It is fear.

Jesus prophesied that toward the end of time the hearts of men would fail them for fear. Many people drop dead out of sheer fright and terror.

Phobia is the Greek word for fear. The dictionary lists over 700 different kinds of phobias. Acrophobia is a fear of high places; claustrophobia, a fear of tight, closed places; agoraphobia, a fear of open places, also a fear of crowds; ergophobia, a fear of work (many are in that category), and even phobophobia, which is a fear of fear!

Even for the follower of Jesus Christ there are fears. People fear losing their health, their wealth, their friends, their family, their position. Second Timothy has an antidote for fear:

> Wherefore I put thee in remembrance that thou stir up the gift of God which is in thee by the putting on of hands. For God hath not given us the spirit of fear, but of power and of love and of a sound mind. Be not thou therefore ashamed of the testimony of our Lord, nor of me his prisoner: but be thou partaker of the afflictions of the gospel according to the power of God (2 Tim. 1:6-8).

Let me caution you. All fear is not bad. Certain kinds of fear are productive. The fact is: some fear is of God Himself.

Franklin Delano Roosevelt, shortly after becoming president in 1933, declared: "We have nothing to fear but fear itself." "That ain't necessarily so." There is plenty to fear besides fear. As long as there are rattlesnakes and poison spiders and drunken drivers and rapists and terrorists and muggers—and more—I would make not a statement like that.

If we had no fear, we would be liable to injure ourselves constantly or either kill ourselves. Fear can be helpful and therapeutic. God has given us a sense of caution that can protect and preserve us.

On one occasion Jesus literally told us to fear: "And fear not them which kill the body, but are not able to kill the soul: but rather fear him which is able to destroy both soul and body in hell" (Matt. 10:28). If you are not saved, that is a legitimate fear for you. The unsaved person should live in a constant state of foreboding.

The Bible also speaks concerning "the fear of the Lord." That is a desirable fear. The Book of Proverbs counsels that "The fear of the Lord is the beginning of wisdom" (1:7). You do not have a modicum of wisdom unless you fear the Lord.

To fear the Lord does not mean you cow and cringe before Him. It indicates a reverential awe and worship before Him. You are to have a holy respect for Him. At the same time the Christian should fear what could happen to his life, influence, and testimony.

A smart electrician is going to fear electricity if he is going to have longevity on the job. That power can kill him, so he ought to take precautions when he works with electricity. Sometimes he trembles when he thinks about the destructive force of that power. An airline pilot, although he may possess confidence, will have a form of fear that causes him to double-check all the instruments. He recognizes that a wrong decision could result in death—his, his passengers, and possibly others. An airline pilot told me there are two kinds of pilots—"bold pilots and old pilots, but there are no old bold pilots."

The conscientious pharmacist fears mixing up the prescriptions. For instance, he could accidentally give a capsule to raise one's blood pressure to a patient who already has runaway high blood pressure! Fear.

There is no competition between fearing the Lord and loving Him. The person who fears the Lord the most loves Him the best.

The fear of the Lord is love on its knees. The fear of the Lord is clean, healthy, and fruitful. But here I am referring to "a spirit of fear." "For God hath not given us the spirit of fear, but of power and of love and of a sound mind."

This is a negative fear we might call a phobia. Many fearful people have scores of phobias they are even afraid to name. Their fears are irrational, often unfounded, and sometimes senselessly insane. The spirit of fear is damaging to the psyche.

Let us look at . . .

THE DESTRUCTIVE POWER OF FEAR

Notice three basic hurts fear can inflict on us. For example, there is *fear* and *forgetfulness*. In verse 6 the apostle reminded Timothy, "Wherefore *I put thee in remembrance* that thou stir up the gift which is in thee by the putting on of my hands."

Timothy was a gifted man, but no doubt he had forgotten his heritage. Paul links Timothy's forgetfulness with fear because the next verse states, "For God hath not given us the spirit of fear."

When you focus on fear, it removes the blue from the skies and hangs crepe paper on the doorknob of your heart. You may fail to understand who you are or what you can do through Christ.

Untold thousands of Christians are immensely gifted and tremendously blessed of God, but they have phobias that stifle them and keep them from receiving all God has in store for them. In fixating on your fear, you tend to forget God and all His blessings.

Friend, do not focus on your fears. Rather, center on Christ.

At the particular time Paul wrote to young Timothy, Tim (and Paul may have called him that for short) probably had nothing specific to be afraid of. Paul, on the other hand, definitely did. Someone was always out to kill him or discredit him. Guess where Paul was when he wrote this. In prison. Verse 8 challenges: "Be not therefore ashamed of the testimony of our Lord, nor of me his prisoner."

Paul was a prisoner of the Lord in a metaphorical sense, in that he was "a bondslave to the Lord Jesus," but he was also a prisoner in the literal sense because he was incarcerated at Rome, maybe even waiting to be executed. Yet, Paul was not afraid.

In verse 12 he testifies: "For the which cause I also suffer these things, nevertheless I am not ashamed, for I know whom I have believed, and am persuaded that he is able to keep that which I have committed unto him against that day." Even though he was in prison under the threat of death, he was jubilant and triumphant. Paul could affirm, "I know whose I am. I know what I have turned over to the Lord. I'm in prison, yes. I am shut up. Guarded twenty-four hours a day. It's all right. I'm OK."

Paul had not forgotten who he was and how great God was. Somehow you can feel the breath of heaven blowing through Paul's prison cell.

If you are obsessed by fear and overcome by it, you have forgotten who God is and what He has done for you.

So, fear is linked to forgetfulness, forgetting the God who has bought us with His own blood. Now let us look at *fear* and *failure* in verse 8. "Be not therefore ashamed of the testimony of our Lord nor of me his prisoner."

There is the possibility that Timothy had failed to share Christ and also to stand up for the apostle Paul. Why? Paul was in prison and perhaps Timothy was afraid of what could also happen to him. Maybe fear had shut his mouth, had momentarily paralyzed him.

When we ought to succeed in our spiritual lives, many of us fail for one glaring reason—because we have listened to the felon of fear, the devil, rather than to God, and that fear has frozen and immobilized us. It matters not how gifted or talented we are.

I heard of a man whose farm was failing, whose wife needed surgery, whose bills were past due, and the banks would not lend him a cent. He decided that all he could do was rob a bank. He tried to gain enough courage. He paced back and forth around the bank. He had a bag for the teller to put the money in and a pistol with which to frighten him/her. He was literally scared to death and tried to talk himself out of the escapade. He was all "conflustragrated," as the Kingfish used to say. Shakily, the farmer shoved the gun at the teller, instead of the bag. Then he pointed that floppy bag at the teller and stammered, "Don't stick with me—this is a mess up!"

That's what fear will do for you.

Too many believers hide their God-given abilities and gifts under a bushel. Why? Because of fear. Sadly, many of them will lose those talents and abilities if they are not exercised for God's glory. It is a worldly sounding expression but none the less true, "If you don't use it, you'll lose it." Jesus taught, "For unto whomsoever much is given, of him shall be much required" (Luke 12:48*b*).

All around us are people whose lives are being strangled by the boa constrictors of fear. They are hardly able to function because they are tied in the knots of fear. Fear is at the core of their lives. When fear dominates, there is no room for Christ Who comforts us: "These things have I spoken unto you, that in me ye might have peace. In the world ye shall have tribulation: but be of good cheer; I have overcome the world" (John 16:33).

Our Lord presented the parable of the talents and how He gave each person different talents. The man with one talent alibied, with sullen lips protruding, "I took your talent, and I hid it in the ground because I was afraid" (see Matt. 25:14-30). "I was afraid." It breaks my heart to think of all the unutilized talent in our churches. Many will never use those gifts because they are afraid. Because of that, people are ashamed of the testimony of our Lord.

I believe every true believer wants to be a soul-winner. Why is it, then, that only two or three out of every one hundred Christians ever knowingly lead a soul to Christ? In my own denomination, why does it take forty-five Baptists to reach one soul for Jesus? The late Dr. Roland Q. Leavell, author of the classic *Evangelism: Christ's Imperative Commission,* wrote that fear was the number-one cause for Christians not witnessing. The icy fingers of fear strangle their witness.

So many are deathly afraid of failure and the embarrassment that may accompany it. If you believe you are going to fail, the chances are you will. Have you tried driving behind a person who was so fearful he was going to catch every red light that he did? Many grown people are like the little kids who played the game of "step on a crack, break your mama's back." So they would walk for miles and gingerly try to miss the cracks, never looking up to see the sky.

They program themselves, because of fear, for failure. They can't win for losing. Their favorite phrase is, "I can't." And they can't sure enough. Their built-in fear projects upon them, and they make constant negative confessions. Like the late Hank Williams, Sr., who died at the age of twenty-nine, opined: "Don't worry none 'cause things ain't gonna get no better nohow."

You may think that only weak people are fearful. Right? Not so. Strong persons are oftentimes profoundly afraid. At one time Julius Caesar remarked that even the shouts of his enemies were music to his ears. But he was terribly afraid of thunder. When it vaguely looked like a storm was brewing, he would begin to shiver and shake.

Peter the great, considered "the greatest" czar of Russia, was terrified to cross a bridge. He would tremble in his boots as he stepped onto any bridge. People, even those considered mighty otherwise, can be obsessed and possessed by fear.

Have you ever been neutralized by fear? You had an incomparable opportunity, but you were afraid, and that opportunity has now disappeared. Because of your fear, will it be written of you, "The saddest words of tongue or pen are these—it might have been"?

Fear and *forgetfulness*. *Fear* and *failure*. And also *fear* and *frailty*.

It is now widely known that fear can literally sicken us and weaken our bodies. Paul advised Timothy, "Drink no longer water, but use a little wine for thy stomach's sake and thine often infirmities."

More than likely Timothy was sickly and was probably having stomach disorders. Back in those days internal medicine was almost nonexistent. Maybe Timothy had a peptic ulcer or colitis. Was he afraid because he was sick? Maybe. It is perhaps more reasonable to surmise that he was sickly because he was afraid. His sickness could have been precipitated by his fear. Many Christians are inclined toward a fearful disposition, and he was sick from his fears.

One prominent American internist observed at a roundtable discussion on psychosomatic medicine: "In spite of what they say, 90 percent of the chronic patients who see today's physicians have one common problem. Their trouble did not start with a cough or chest pain or hyperacidity. In 90 percent of the cases the first symptom was fear."

All types of problems can be created by fear. Others can be inflamed because of worry and fear, for instance in the case of arthritis. You can worry yourself into a hospital or institution. At times people are literally worried stiff!

Worry is strongly tied to fear. They are noxious first cousins who feed on each other. People who are carrying the burdensome load of worry and fear often suffer strokes and heart attacks. It is estimated that the vast majority of physical illnesses are caused by fear, stress, strain, and worry.

Fear in your life is like sand in machinery. Faith in your life is like oil—it lubricates the life. But fear will do to you what grit does to machinery.

Now I have touched on *the destructive power of the spirit of fear*. Positively, I move to . . .

THE DELIVERING POWER OF THE SPIRIT OF FAITH

Be thankful that Paul does not stop with the destructive power of the spirit of fear, but he centers on deliverance. Not only is he presenting the answer to Timothy but also to you. Second Timothy 1:7 is a high-water mark: "For God hath not given us the spirit of fear, but of power and of love and of a sound mind."

Here are three elements freely given to us by the Lord—*power, love,* and a *sound mind*. With these you can have a future free from the bondage of fear. Now you will notice I did not write "a future free from fear." No. I am thinking of the enslavement of fear until our fear blocks out the sun and darkens even the light of our lives. I repeat: certain kinds of fear are essential. Healthy fear can be good and productive.

Several years ago our phone rang in the middle of the night. It was one of my sons' roommates in college at Waco, Texas. He asked, "Mr. Rogers, isn't David supposed to be coming back to school today?" "Yes," I replied, "He left here early this morning. He should've had plenty of time to be there by now."

It was after midnight, and I thought, *What could have happened?* "Well, Mr. Rogers, I just thought I ought to let you know he's not here." My mind began to run amok. I thought about the rattletrap car he was driving. It was a dark, stormy night, at least in Memphis. *Maybe he's had a blowout. Or he's been robbed. Or he's out of gas, or he's in a wreck, or he's been abducted.* I thought of a thousand and one things.

My son's roommate continued, "Mr. Rogers, you have any idea where he is?" I answered, "No. Please call me in an hour and let me know if he's in." Early in the morning he called back and tersely reported, "He's not here."

Hours before then he should have been there! I asked myself, *How am I going to find him in hundreds of miles of road? What am I going to do? Who can I contact?* I felt the spirit of fear icing me over. There I was. I had preached to thousands, "Fear not." I had encouraged them not to be afraid. At that moment I put this question to myself, *Why doesn't your sermon work?*

I preached that sermon to myself, and it still did not seem to allay my fear. It was still there. I grilled myself, *Am I a hypocrite? Have I been preaching something that's not true? Why, oh why, am I afraid right now?*

Then I realized that fear, as I had analyzed it, was a legitimate fear. God gave me a valid fear which dictated, "If there is anything you can do, do it now. Move into action. Don't go back to bed if there is something you can do to make a difference." In that case there was nothing I could do but pray and wait, at least right then. So, I committed it to the Lord.

Soon I found out that our son had gone to Dallas. There he had met a fellow looking for directions. My son had been driving all over Big D trying to help that man out. Son figured Daddy would not know what time he would arrive in Waco, so what Daddy didn't know wouldn't hurt him. But Daddy found out—and it did hurt Daddy.

There is justified fear—fear of the fire, of electricity, of poison snakes and spiders, fear of the fiend who would harm your wife or your children, and fear for your son who had seemingly disappeared.

What I am cautioning you against is that non-productive, negative spirit of fear. Legitimate fear is like a thunderstorm. The lightning flashes, the thunder rolls, the water pours down, and then the storm passes. The clouds roll back, and the sun shines through once again.

But the spirit of fear is like a constant darkness. A steady drizzle, an ever-present fog. You exist in it. It covers, smothers, and stifles you.

That sort of spirit is not of the Lord. God has not given that to you. There is also a difference between worry and fear. I realize I had begun to worry about our son, so I confessed to the Lord, "I can't worry. I must leave it in Your hands." And I did.

I suggest three qualities that will enable you to have a future free from the bondage of fear.

First, God Has Endued Us with Power.

"God has not given us the spirit of fear, but of power . . ." Jesus promised that we would be endued with power from on high. "But ye shall receive power, after that the Holy Ghost is come upon you . . . " (Acts 1:8). He is talking about the power of the Holy Spirit.

So often we are afraid because we do not believe we have the necessary resources to face the challenges before us. We do not have the spiritual equipment with which to face the foe, the devil himself. If I understand that resident within me is a power greater than any foe anywhere, I do not have to be afraid. Paul calls Christ "the power of God." "Greater is he that is in you than he that is in the world" (1 John 4:4).

Many children have experienced fright at school, on the playground, in their neighborhoods, or even in the home. Most of us had at least one bully who followed us. We were afraid to walk home from school. There was this certain kid who always picked on me. Every day this mean old bully stalked my footsteps. I was scared almost speechless. One day I decided I had had enough, so I turned around and told *her*, "You leave me alone!" (Ha!)

If you have the spirit of fear, it is because you are not centered in the Lord. You have failed to remember the gift of God in you. God is with you all the time. The Holy Spirit is your Bodyguard. He walks with us, and He communes with us, and we have blessed fellowship.

The psalmist sang it: "The lord is my light and my salvation, whom shall I fear?" (Ps. 27:1*a*). Since the Lord is my light and my salvation, there is no one to fear. "The Lord is the strength of my life; of whom shall I be afraid?" (Ps. 27:1*b*).

The fear of the Lord removes all other fears. The man who can kneel before God can stand before any man.

I want you to make a mental checklist. Am I remembering God's power shown in me? Do I know just how great my God is? Only glance at your problems but gaze at your God. The fear of man made

Saul a coward. The fear of God made David a hero when he marched out to slay Goliath.

Second, God Has Enriched Us with the Spirit of Love.

We have not only the spirit of power but also *the spirit of love*. Love is a mighty force in dealing with fear. But how does love combat fear?

> There is no fear in love; but perfect love casteth out fear: because fear hath torment. He that feareth is not made perfect in love (1 John 4:18).

For a long time that verse bothered me. It was of practically no help to me, because I thought it meant that if I loved God perfectly I would not be afraid—ever. I thought to myself, *My, I don't do anything perfectly except sin. so how is that going to help me?* But that does not mean that if I love God perfectly I will not be afraid. It actually means that I do not have to be afraid *because God loves me perfectly*.

The Living Bible amplifies beautifully the statement of 1 John 4:18: "We need have no fear of someone who loves us perfectly." That is so comforting to folks like me.

His perfect love eliminates all dread of what He might do to us. If we are afraid as Christians, it is because we are fearful of what God might do to us or either allow to happen to us. If we fear, that shows we are not fully convinced that He really loves us.

When we see on the one hand God's mighty power and on the other hand God's mighty love, then fears seem to melt away. I still remember that chorus we sang as children: "Rolled away, rolled away, rolled away, Every burden of my heart rolled away."

God endues us with power. He enriches us with love. Now I rest in that love. You and I can pray, "Lord, no matter what happens to me I know that You love me. And because You love me, and because You are all-powerful, "All things work together for good to them who love God, to them who are the called according to his purpose" (Rom. 8:28).

God *endues with power, enriches with love,* and also . . .

God Has Enlightened Us with a Sound Mind.

This phrase "sound mind" indicates that God has given us discipline, self-control, and a discerning spirit. Wise discretion is the ticket. Stop right here. So much of what we are afraid of is not on the basis of reality but because the deceiver, the devil, has induced us to be afraid.

The motivational speaker and best-selling author Zig Ziglar says that fear, F-E-A-R, is often False Evidence which Appears Real. In many instances the devil causes us to be afraid when there is nothing to be afraid of. Nelson Price, in his book *Shadows We Run From,* tells about running for ninety-nine yards for a touchdown, all the while trying to escape his own shadow. We spend a good deal of time running from our shadows.

God gives us a sound mind. We are able to look at our fear in the light of God's Word. Sometimes we have to grab ourselves by the nape of the neck and make ourselves analyze the situation. You have to look past what might happen to you at the immediate moment and recognize that God is ultimately victorious.

That is what Paul did in 1 Timothy 1:12: "For which cause I also suffer these things, nevertheless I am not ashamed for I know whom I have believed and am persuaded that he is able to keep that which I have committed unto him against that day."

Timothy may have been ashamed of the testimony of the Lord. But he came around. He was not blown away by the sinister minister of fear, the devil.

For a quarter of a century after World War II incidents like this were occurring. All over the Pacific, Japanese soldiers were being found holed up, thinking the war was still on as late as 1970. One soldier stayed in a cave for twenty-eight years in the jungles of Guam. He ate frogs, rats, and whatever he could rustle up. For all those years he was a prisoner of fear, fearful that the Japanese would find out he had deserted and fearful of the hated Americans. The war was over, and

Americans were driving Hondas and Toyotas, and vacationing to Tokyo.

Listen. The war is over, and Jesus is the Victor. He has won. "It is finished," he cried from the Cross. He has offered us amnesty and forgiveness. We can all go home. The enemy, Satan, does not want you to know that. He wants to keep you holed up in your cave of fear.

Would you believe that many people do not come to God because they are afraid of Him? They fear Him unhealthily, thinking negatively about Him.

"But there is no fear in love, for perfect love casteth out fear, for fear hath torment."

"Fear not" (Luke 2:10).

9. No Doubt About It

Oh, may I cry when body parts with spirit,
"I do not doubt," so listening worlds may hear it
With my last breath. —Ella Wheeler Wilcox

Doubting Thomas was not confined to the New Testament. All around us are those who doubt, even Christians who have followed Christ for decades. Many a believer is hampered in his witness because he spends considerable time wondering about his relationship to God.

We often speak about "a know-so salvation." Wouldn't it be marvelous if all believers could sing, and mean it, "I know, I know. There's no doubt about it. He lives in my heart, and I'm gonna shout it."

The apostle John penned his Gospel that we might be saved. "But these are written, that ye might believe that Jesus is the Christ, the Son of God; and that believing ye might have life through his name" (John 20:21).

The Epistle of 1 John was written to aid the believer in *knowing he is saved*. Repeatedly he uses the word "know"—that "ye may know." It is plain that we can know. An interesting exercise is to circle the word *know* in 1 John. You will be amazed.

"These things have I written unto you that believe on the name of the Son of God; that ye may *know* that ye have eternal life, and that ye may believe on the name of the Son of God" (5:13). First John clearly teaches that we can *know* we are saved, we have passed from death unto life, we have been born again. It not only tells us we can know we are saved but also that one can be saved and doubt it.

If one could be saved and not doubt it, why did John write this Epistle? The overriding purpose of 1 John is to help doubting Christians have assurance of their salvation—or as one little boy put it, "*insurance* of salvation."

So many believers worry, "If I doubt my salvation, then it must mean I am not saved." Indeed it may mean that you are truly saved and that you care enough about your soul to be concerned, to be asking questions. You see, we doubt only what we tend to believe.

By no means am I encouraging you to have doubt. I am merely making a point that there is a bright side to doubt. Doubt is to your spirit what pain is to your body. When you have a pain, does it imply you are already dead? Of course not! It actually means you are alive.

> My faith is all a doubtful thing,
> Wove on a doubtful loom,
> Until there comes, each showery spring,
> A cherry tree in bloom;
>
> And Christ, who died upon a tree
> That death hath stricken bare,
> Comes beautifully back to me,
> In blossoms everywhere.
>
> —David Morton

It is possible to be saved and to know it. In fact, that ought to be the norm for the believer in Jesus Christ, but it is also possible to be saved and doubt it from time to time. Else John never would have treated this subject.

This chapter has a twofold purpose—to assist those who are saved but may occasionally doubt and to touch those who have no right to know they are saved, because they never have been. If you have never received Christ, it is my prayer you will.

Once a woman boasted to D. L. Moody, that powerful evangelist of yesteryear: "Mr. Moody, I have been saved for twenty-five years, and

I have never had a single doubt." Moody replied, "Madam, I doubt that you're saved. That would be like somebody saying, 'We've been married fifty years and never had an argument!' I doubt if they have been married."

Moody also declared, "I've never known anyone who was any good in the service of Christ who did not, first of all, have the assurance of his or her salvation."

Only when you settle the future can you concentrate on the present. The chronic doubters seldom make an impact for Christ because they consume time and energy worrying about their spiritual condition. John Wesley tried and tried to serve Christ, but he was never truly effective until he had his Aldersgate experience, when he "felt strangely warmed" by the Holy Spirit.

I have never known a mighty soul-winner who was always doubting his salvation. How can you invite people to follow you toward Jesus if you don't know where you're going? Think about it. Those who count the most for Christ must be able to testify:

> For the which cause I also suffer these things: nevertheless I am not ashamed: for I know whom I have believed, and am persuaded that he is able to keep that which I have committed unto him against that day (2 Tim. 1:2).

Yes, you can doubt. But you should not remain in constant doubt. If you do, and doubt is persistent, perhaps you are not saved. There is a debate as to whether doubt can be beneficial. If it is helpful, it is such only in one direction. Your doubt can make you long for assurance and sweet peace. Armed with confidence you can then move onward for the Lord Jesus.

There is no doubt about it: you must deal with your doubt until you can emphatically confess, "I know whom I have believed."

First John presents the signs of salvation. How can you know? How can you be sure? Let me set forth three basic tests which will help you determine whether or not you are saved. Number one is:

THE COMMANDMENT TEST

First John 2:3-4 is crucial:

> And hereby we do *know* that we *know* him, if we keep his commandments. He that saith, I *know* him, and keepeth not his commandments, is a liar, and the truth is not in him.

Although John was called "the apostle of love," he certainly could let the hammer down about these matters. In other words, "If you claim to know Christ, to have an intimate salvation experience with Him, and you do not keep His commandments and do what He instructs, you are a liar." Wow!

He was not only straightforward but also logical. His argument continues in verses 5 and 6:

> But whoso keepeth his word, in him verily is the love of God perfected: hereby *know* we that we are in him. He that saith he abideth in him ought himself also so to walk, even as *he* walked.

There is no point in our trying to make this sound difficult. If I am in Christ, and Christ is in me, then I am going to be walking as Jesus walked. And how did He walk? According to the commandments of the Word of God, that's how.

"Wait a minute, Adrian," you may retort. "We are supposed to keep His commandments, and that will prove whether or not we are saved. But I'm not certain I've kept them all. I've fallen short from time to time." Now, no one would claim that since the day of his salvation he has never transgressed even one of God's commandments, would he? I think not, unless that person were rather deranged.

So, we appear to have a problem here. John emphasizes that if we know God, we will keep His commandments. The key is found in the word "keep." Ron Dunn has pointed out that in the original language it was a sailor's or mariner's term. It was based upon the fact that in those days the sailors steered by the stars. John was borrowing that term. He means we are to steer by the commandments. Those mariners did not always steer correctly. Sometimes they missed the mark.

They oversteered. They were sometimes blown off course, or they fell asleep while on duty. But the aim and desire of the mariner's life was to steer by those stars. That is the case with every born-again Christian—to steer by what God says.

Here John does not have sinless perfection in mind, but he is stressing that, if a person is saved, he will want to live right in holiness and righteousness.

How can you be sure you are saved? Put this down in your book: *it will grieve a Christian when he sins*. It severely grieved David when he sinned against God. Despite his sins of adultery, murder, lying, covetousness, cheating, and more, he prayed, "Restore unto me the joy of thy salvation; and uphold me with thy free spirit" (Ps. 51:12). It tore up the apostle Peter's heart when he denied his Lord and warmed his hands at the devil's fire.

> And Peter remembered the word of Jesus, which said unto him, Before the cock crow, thou shalt deny me thrice. And he went out, and wept bitterly (Matt. 26:75).

There is an ancient story about a Roman officer who wanted to persecute and punish a certain Christian. He called together his advisors and inquired, "What can we do to punish him? What about confiscating his goods?"

"No," replied one of his advisors, "he doesn't have any of this world's goods, and anyhow he claims to have riches in glory, and we cannot put our hands on those."

"What about putting him into solitary confinement then?"

"That would not work either, Sire, because he has a friend that sticks closer than a brother, and he will commune with that friend in prayer."

"Well, we'll kill him."

"Sire, he will simply die and go to heaven. There he will be in the companionship of his Lord, and he would love that."

Now irked, the Roman official commanded, "Then what can we do to make him suffer? I demand to know."

"Sire, if you really want to make him suffer hideously, make him sin, because if he sins, he will suffer!"

Any genuine Christian will suffer when he sins. Dabbling in sin, a genuine Christian feels out of place like a sore thumb. He will hurt as He feels God's love and conviction wooing him back into full fellowship with his tender, loving Lord.

The Psalmist cried out, "I delight to do thy will, O God." You will not want to sin because sin grieves not only God but you as well. You will yearn to keep God's commandments because disobedience and rebellion are not to be part of your new nature in Him.

If you were privileged to have a loving, sharing family life as a child, do you recall those times when you intentionally or unintentionally disobeyed your mother or father? You were fearful not only of punishment but of the embarrassment and shame of displeasing and hurting your parents. Their discovery of your misdeed was punishment enough. Do you remember running to them and, in tears, begging for forgiveness and restoration? You did not want to offend those you loved. It is like that toward our Lord.

Can you pray with the poet . . . ?

Have Thine own way, Lord!
Have Thine own way!
Thou art the Potter, I am the clay!
Mold me and make me after Thy will,
While I am waiting, yielded and still.

Have Thine own way, Lord!
Have Thine own way!
Search me and try me, Master, today!
Whiter than snow, Lord, Wash me just now,
As in Thy presence humbly I bow.

—Adelaide A. Proctor

There was *the commandment test,* and second there is:

THE COMPANION TEST

> If a man say, I love God, and hateth his brother, he is a liar: for he that loveth not his brother whom he hath seen, how can he love God whom he hath not seen? (1 John 4:20).
>
> We know that we have passed from death unto life, because we love the brethren. He that loveth not his brother abideth in death (3:14).
>
> Whosoever believeth that Jesus is the Christ is born of God: and every one that loveth him that begat loveth him also that is begotten of him (5:1).

If you are genuinely born again, if you are saved, you are going to love the brethren—and the "sistern," too. Through the bonds of faith you will cherish your brothers and sisters in Christ. It follows as the daylight comes after the dawn.

That is one birthmark of the believer. When you are saved you are going to want affiliation and affinity with the saints. The Apostle John, tradition has it, was perhaps allowed to leave the Isle of Patmos and return to his pastorate at Ephesus. Almost blind and deaf, he would be carried into the meetings of the believers. He would repeat again and again, "The fellowship of the saints, Oh, the fellowship of the saints!"

How often we have heard professing Christians comment, "I can worship God just as well by myself as you can in church." Many of them, when asked where they attend church, answer, "Well, I'm just a Christian. I just go here and there. After all, I'm non-denominational or interdenominational."

Jesus suffered and died for the church, shedding His own precious blood. If the church was and is that important to our Lord and Savior, how should we feel about it? You know the answer. Samuel J. Stone expressed it well:

> The church's one foundation
> Is Jesus Christ her Lord;
> She is His new creation,
> By Spirit and the Word:

From heav'n He came and sought her
To be His holy bride,
With His own blood he bought her,
And for her life He died.

The Bible candidly admonishes us not to forsake "the assembling of ourselves together, as the manner of some is; but exhorting one another: and so much the more, as ye see the day [the second coming] approaching" (Heb. 10:25). Yes, the church is the church, whether assembled or unassembled, but we are to assemble together for many reasons—first of all because God commands it. And we need one another.

It is interesting that the word "saint" is never used in the singular in the New Testament. It is always "saints"—plural. This emphasizes the import of our collective witness for Christ. I am always amazed when I hear professing Christians claim that they love Christ but they abhor other Christians. That makes no sense at all.

Sometimes our brothers and sisters are less than paragons of Christian virtue. Peter and Paul and Barnabas and Silas were far from perfect. They had faults which were spelled out in the New Testament. It is not always easy to like some of the brethren, but we are to *love* them. If we are honest, most of us would admit that at times members of our families irk and upset us. But we love them—I pray that we do—in spite of their foibles.

"We Are Family" was the title of a song several years ago. Yes, we are family in the Lord. An unknown author has mused:

To dwell above with those we love,
Oh, that will be glory,
But to live here below with those we know,
Well, that's another story!

Our brethren are still human beings. When they were saved that did not mean all their peccadilloes and idiosyncrasies flew out the window. Neither does it imply that all of them have glowing, loving personalities and would win the prize for Mr. or Miss Congeniality. I repeat: if we are saved we are going to love our fellow Christians.

Examine John's thinking. Why is love an earmark of your being born again? It is the nature of a Christian because he has assumed God's nature—and God is love.

> Beloved, let us love one another: for love is of God; and every one that loveth is born of God, and knoweth God (4:7).

Note the development of this idea. Love is of God, and every person who truly loves is born of God and knows God. Since God's nature is love, when one wants to describe Him, he speaks of God as *love*.

When you are born of God you share His nature. It is this transparently simple. If you are born of God, it will follow that you will love your brothers and sisters in the Lord. You will love the church of the Lord Jesus, which is composed of your born-again brethren.

So, because of God's nature, the Christian's inherited nature is love. Second of all, love is the chief characteristic of the church. The Bible refers to the church as the bride of Christ and the body of Christ.

"Why do you love God?" asked the teacher. The little girl thought about that and said, "Teacher, I guess it just runs in our family,"[1] Loving God and His church just runs in the family.

The Church Is His Body.

> And he hath put all things in subjection under His feet, and gave Him as head over all things to the church, which is His body, the fullness of Him who fills all in all (Eph. 1:22-23, NASB).
>
> He is also the head of the body, the church; and He is the beginning, the first born from the dead; so that He Himself might come to have first place in everything. Now I rejoice in my sufferings for your sake, and in my flesh I do my share on behalf of His body (which is the church), in filling up that which is lacking in Christ's afflictions (Col. 1:18,24, NASB).

Through the years many people have been alibiing, "Jesus *yes* but the church *no*." How ridiculous. Christ is the Head of the church. Such a cop-out is akin to saying, "My head *yes* but my body *no*." The church and Jesus are not identical, but they are inseparable. Separate my head from my body, and what do you have? Death. Christ is the Head; we are His body.

For a person to proclaim, "I love Jesus, but I don't love His church," is unmitigated foolishness. If you love Jesus, you are going to love what He loves. If you honestly love a person, you are going to love him/her in body, soul, mind, and spirit—in toto. You will accept the whole person. You're not going to blurt out, "Hey, I love your head, but I can't stand your body!" The body may have imperfections—scars, moles, wrinkles, cellulite—but if you love a person, you will love his head and his body.

Then we ought to remember that . . .

The Church Is His Bride.

In Ephesians 5:22-31 Paul refers to godly relations between husband and wife, but his major purpose is found in verses 32-33:

> This is a great mystery: but I speak concerning Christ and the church. Nevertheless let every one of you in particular so love his wife even as himself; and the wife see that she reverence her husband.

Throughout the New Testament, down to the last verses of Revelation, the church is called the bride of the Lord Jesus. "And the Spirit and the bride say, Come. . . ." (Rev. 22:17*a*).

If you are the right kind of husband, you would sacrifice your life for your wife. You can kick me if you have to, but leave my wife, my bride, alone. She is my beloved, my wife, my bride. I will defend her to the death.

It makes no sense for a person to claim, "I love Jesus," and then denigrate or ignore His Bride. Don't tell me you love the Lord if you don't love His Bride, the church.

The Church Is God's Building.

How can you know whether you are saved? If you love the brethren, if you love the church. John is not speaking about a building constructed of bricks, mortar, stone, and metal. He is referring to the saints of God who worship there. Paul wrote: "Ye are God's husbandry; ye are God's building" (1 Cor. 3:9). His building (God's people) is where He dwells and where you will find fellowship.

We have dealt with the *commandment test*, the *companion* (or love) *test*, and now we reach the *commitment test*.

THE COMMITMENT TEST

> He that believeth on the Son of God hath the witness in himself: he that believeth not God hath made him a liar; because he believeth not the record that God gave of his Son. And this is the record, that God hath given to us eternal life, and this life is in his Son. He that hath the Son hath life; and he that hath not the Son of God hath not life. These things have I written unto you that believe on the name of the Son of God; that ye may *know* that ye have eternal life, and that ye may believe on the name of the Son of God (5:10-13).

Why call this the *commitment test?* I could name it the *belief* test, but our English word "believe" is sometimes not forceful enough. People in our day have come to associate *belief* or *believe* with intellectual belief or assent. For instance, I believe that Henry Wadsworth Longfellow lived, but I am not *committed* to him. I am not trusting him for this or that. I like several of his poems, but I am not believing in him to guide and pilot my life.

The Bible word translated *believe*—"Believe on the Lord Jesus Christ, and thou shalt be saved"—means a trust, a commitment. Are you by faith committed to Jesus Christ? Are you totally counting on Him, banking on Him? New Testament belief is far beyond mere intellectual, head assent.

This may sound controversial, but I will stand by it. Nowhere in the Bible do I find where you have to look back to a past experience for the assurance of salvation. I have often heard that if you cannot name the exact moment of the exact minute of the exact hour of the exact day of the exact month of the exact year, you are not saved. But I honestly have never been able to locate that in the pages of God's Word.

The Bible does not say, "He that *believed*"—past tense. It says rather, "He that *believes*"—present tense. If you are believing for salvation right now, you did believe sometime in the past. Right? But if you are not believing now, I have no idea what happened to you back there, but whatever it was, was not salvation. Salvation is in the present tense.

With all three tests—*the commandment test, the companion test,* and *the commitment test*—it is the same. A person keeps the commandments—now, in the present tense. He loves the brethren—in the present tense. "He that believeth." "He that loveth." "He that keepeth"—in the present tense.

If you have done soul-winning visitation, you will run into too many people like this. I will call him Rube. Rube hasn't darkened the door of a church in decades. He, for all practical purposes, is living for the devil. If you invite him to church you might as well be talking to a concrete slab. So, you endeavor to lead him to Christ, and he begins his pitch, "Why, I got saved when I was nine years old back there at Mount Pisgah Baptist Church. I'm saved."

I wouldn't want to be in his shoes at the judgment! From all evidence, what happened at Mount Pisgah probably was not salvation, but all of these years he has been hiding behind that day he walked the aisle. Do you believe in Christ for salvation right this moment? Do you have the witness within that you are a born-again, blood-bought child of God?

First John 5:10 speaks about this present salvation: "He that believeth on the Son of God hath the witness in himself: . . ." It is a right-now salvation. Do you have that "blessed assurance, Jesus is mine" in your heart? Paul wrote: "The Spirit itself beareth witness with our spirit, that we are the children of God" (Rom. 8:16). That witness is the inner assurance that one is saved. Salvation is not some thirty-second experience that you get over. Ron Dunn has also said, "You are not a post stuck in the ground. You are a tree planted, and that growth has to continue throughout life."

It reminds me of the couple for whom I performed a wedding ceremony. When they finished with the "I do's," the boy—and he was a boy—asked, "Is it all over?" I replied, "No, Son, it's only beginning."

Of course, I am happy for you if you can name the precise time when you were saved. I, too, remember when I settled the matter between God and me. But that is not nearly as important as knowing that you have Christ in your heart *right this moment*. If you are saved, there was a time and place, whether or not you can pinpoint it.

You might inquire, "But how could I be saved and not know the time?" Let me ask you this—How could some people be born physically and not know the date of their birth? They are alive, but many people are not sure when they were born the first time. Many people do not even have a birth certificate and do not even know where to request one. The humorist of a bygone era, Will Rogers, did not know the date of his birth. He wanted a passport to travel overseas, so he contacted a government official, and he asked Rogers, "Where is your birth certificate? We need one."

Rogers answered, "What for?"

The reply was: "As a proof of your birth."

Rogers said, "I'm here, ain't I? That's a better proof of birth, ain't it?" What would be better proof of one's birth than standing there in the flesh or a piece of paper?

The best proof you are saved is right where you are. Are you now, this moment, trusting Christ as your personal Savior? Do you attest to that inner assurance witnessed by the Holy Spirit? God's Spirit will bear witness with your spirit, "Yes, you are saved."

There is *the commandment test*. Do you long to live a holy life? Do you no longer habitually practice sin? There is *the companion test*. Do you actually love the church of the Lord Jesus? And there is *the commitment test*. Loving the brethren and keeping the commandments do not save, but they are the birthmarks of the new birth. It is faith in Christ, and that alone, that saves. Have you committed your heart and life, by faith, to Christ? These are the birthmarks of the new birth, being born again.

If you are not sure, apply these tests. If you continue to have doubts, then pray to the Lord, "I am not sure, but I want to be. As best as I can, I ask you, Lord, to forgive my sins and give me peace and assurance within. I come to you now. Save me." And He will. Jesus promised, "Him that cometh to me I will in no wise cast him out" (John 6:37*a*).

Then you can sing with the blind poet, Fanny J. Crosby:

> Blessed assurance, Jesus is mine,
> Oh, what a foretaste of glory divine!
> Heir of salvation, purchase of God,
> Born of His Spirit, wash'd in His blood.
>
> This is my story, this is my song,
> Praising my Savior all the day long.
> This is my story, this is my song,
> Praising my Savior all the day long.

NOTES

1. J. Winston Pearce, *To Brighten Each Day* (Nashville: Broadman Press, 1983), p. 76.

10. Starlight at Midnight

The life of men is an arrow's flight,
Out of darkness into light.
—Richard Henry Stoddard

Matthew Arnold of Great Britain, a Christian essayist of the nineteenth century, wrote a book entitled *Sweetness and Light*. Unfortunately, not all is sweetness and light. We wish it were. Many Christians came up under preaching and teaching that presented a "Pollyanna Gospel," that nothing bad would ever happen to them. "Come to Jesus," they heard, "and all difficulties and problems will vanish." For this reason, many a Christian is distraught and disillusioned when periods of confusion and frustration, yes, bewilderment, steep him in anxious upset.

Here I want to wrestle with a condition which will develop in your life, if indeed it has not done so. Believe it or not, if you live long enough, you will discover yourself in deep despair and darkness. There will be times of difficulty—when absolutely nothing makes sense.

When bewilderment enshrouds us, and perplexity comes, we are going to question God and ask, "Why, why, why?" When that happens, when confusion foggily sets in, all of our little formulae, outlines, and pat approaches are not going to work. And we are not going to understand what God is up to. We will be going through what the Middle Ages theologian, John of the Cross, called "the dark night of the soul." You will wonder what has happened. You will question whether you have lost your mind. You may even ask where God has gone, because His power and presence seem far removed. We can wear out all of the clichés about that dark night—at your wit's end, up a tree, between a rock and a hard place, at the end of your rope, out of it, wasted, out of touch with reality—and all of them will apply to your miserable condition.

Wait. Why do I deal with this unsavory subject? Why does a doctor talk with you about cancer and heart disease and diabetes? To prepare you. To protect you. To help you parry the worst.

Isaiah understood the dark night of the soul. Hear him:

> Who is among you that heareth the Lord, that obeyeth the voice of his servant, that walketh in darkness, and hath no light? let him trust in the name of the Lord, and stay upon his God. Behold, all ye that kindle a fire, that compass yourself about with sparks: walk in the light of your fire, and in the sparks that ye have kindled. This shall ye have in mine hand; ye shall lie down in sorrow (Isa. 50:10-11).

What Isaiah speaks of is the discipline of darkness. This is not pleasant, but it is essential. Those of my generation remember when medicine tasted terrible. Sometimes it seemed worse than the disease. And do you remember your mother assuring you, "It's good for you. Take it"? Sure you do.

THE POSSIBILITY OF DARKNESS

There is the distinct prospect that dark days and nights will blanket your soul. And that is definitely difficult to understand. Why? Why? Why?

Darkness is not unusual in the life of a Christian. That may sound counter to all you have heard, especially in this day of sugar-coated, *positive this and positive that* preaching and teaching. This darkness may occur in the lives of born-again believers who love the Lord Jesus Christ and wait on Him. I am not referring in this instance to those who walk in constant spiritual darkness, those who are rebellious toward God.

Read the biographies of the saints of God, and you will find, almost without exception, that they suffered periods of deep travail of soul. Many of them plunged so deeply they wondered if God had forsaken them. It happened to Job. If ever a man was godly and faithful to the Almighty, it was he, but he plummeted into the pits. “Darkness” was one of his commonly used words. Job moaned, “He [God] maketh my path darkness.” God was beyond Job’s comprehension, so Job cried repeatedly, “Why?” Job’s life, of course, had a happy ending, but that did not mean he had all of the answers.

Quite often people come to me, asking that question, “Why?” It is sad, but oftentimes I simply do not know why—and have to answer, sometimes to their chagrin, “I don’t know. Somehow we’ll understand it better by and by.” People, especially in the crucible of inscrutable pain and suffering, feel they could survive only if they had more of the answers. Read the Book of Job line on line and precept on precept, and God never did explain Job’s ordeal to him. It was enough that God was with him and that “underneath are the everlasting arms.”

Habakkuk was in the same situation as Job. One of his favorite questions was “why.” At least it is implied almost throughout his prophecy. “Why doest thou show me iniquity, and cause me to behold grievance? for spoiling and violence are before me: and there are that raise up strife and contention” (Hab. 1:3). In the previous verse he virtually wailed, “O Lord, how long shall I cry, and thou wilt not hear! even cry out unto thee of violence, and thou wilt not save!” (v. 2). Habakkuk was in the dilemma of darkness.

John the Baptist was the forerunner of the Lord Jesus and was totally devoted to his Lord. He had announced to the multitudes at Jordan, “Behold the Lamb of God, which taketh away the sin of the world” (John 1:29). John later confessed concerning Jesus, “He must increase, but I must decrease.” But John was arrested for preaching his convictions.

> He [John] was loyal to the Lord Jesus through it all. John was one of the great preachers of all the ages, and was put in prison for denouncing Herod Antipas' wicked marriage with Herodias, and won the enmity of the Pharisees (Luke 3:19). It was a mystery to John why Jesus allowed him to linger in prison, and finally he sent two of his disciples to Jesus to find out, after all, if He was the coming Messiah, or whether another was to come (Matt. 11:2-19; Luke 7:18-35).[1]

Jesus declared that there never was one born of woman greater than John the Baptist—John who had boldly proclaimed a message of repentance. He ate honey but did not preach it. Yet, in the dank, dark prison at Michaerus, John fell into darkness, depression, despair, and perplexity. John had preached the victorious Christ, and yet he was rotting in jail. Finally, John was beheaded at the request of Salome, Herodias's daughter, who requested that John's head be delivered to her on a platter.

The apostle Paul, militant missionary that he was, became blue. In his messages to the Corinthians he spoke of his perplexity. In other words, he simply did not understand. He was bothered and bewildered.

So, if you pass into periods of darkness, you are in good company. You are not by yourself. Remember our text talks about a person who fears the Lord and is obeying Him, yet who has fallen into the doldrums.

Darkness is not *unusual. Darkness is not unfruitful, either*. We cannot figure it out, but there is a purpose behind it. The fruit of the Spirit somehow ripens in the darkness. You will find out that God is moving in your life.

Sometimes your perception can become better in the dark. Remember that you can see the stars only in the darkness. They are there all the time, but you can see them only at night. In the dark the moon is seen snuggling upon the lapel of the night like a gardenia. Those stars nestle in the canopy of space, like a chandelier.

I have never tried this, but I have heard if you are in a deep, dark well in the daytime, you can look up and see the stars shining. There was a book entitled *The View from the Bottom of the Well.* Some truths you can behold only in the chasm of darkness.

Also, there are certain truths you will see better after you have been in the darkness and have reentered the light. Darkness can sharpen your spiritual eyesight.

Once an artist invited a friend to view one of his paintings. He ushered that friend into a room, shut the door, pulled down the shades, and had his friend sit in the darkness for fifteen minutes. Then he requested that the friend look at the painting.

The friend inquired, "Why did you ask me to do such a thing?"

The artist answered, "Because you had too much of the glare of the street in your eyes. Had you seen my painting under those conditions, you would not have been able to appreciate the subtlety of its colors and the nuances of its tones."

Perhaps God lets us endure the darkness because we have been dazzled by the brightness and allurement of the world. He wants us to turn our eyes upon Jesus. He wants us to look full in His wonderful face. He wants the things of earth to grow strangely dim in the light of His glory and grace. We are not always able to do that when we are bedazzled by the trappings and glittering trimmings of this world.

Darkness is *not unfruitful. It is also not unending*. You will emerge from it and be a better person for it. God has a grand purpose for all that He allows to transpire in our lives. *We cannot endure it,* we think. While we are in the darkness we feel that we are going to die, that we will no longer be of value and service to our Lord. But we are going to come through it. "Weeping endureth for a night, but joy cometh in the morning." The same sun that sets is the same one that rises in the morning, and God will indeed lighten the path of his saints.

One of these days the Lord is going to lay hold of the shades of darkness, pin them back with a star, and open the door of the morning, flooding your world with His glory and light. Not now, but perhaps in later years, we will understand.

Merely because it does not make sense to us, does not mean it is senseless in God's economy. "For we know that all things work together for good to them that love God, to those who are called according to his purpose" (Rom. 8:28). One day it might well make sense, and you will exclaim, "Now I see. The dark night was for a purpose. Looking back, no matter how bad it seemed at the time, I would not trade my period of darkness for the floodlights of the world."

When you understand that the darkness is *not unusual, not unfruitful,* and *not unending,* you will feel better about your lot. Then I want you to think about . . .

THE PROCEDURES OF DARKNESS

Literally, Isaiah 50:10-11 instructs us how to handle the darkness when it does come. And if you are a child of God it is assuredly going to come.

The test of your character is how you behave in the dark, not how you conduct yourself in the light. What, then, should we do when the lights go out?

There are three steps you ought to take when the lights go out. One, *you are to look to the Lord*. Verse 10 provides us help at this point: "Who is among you that feareth the Lord, that obeyeth the voice of his servant, that walketh in darkness, and hath no light? let him trust in the name of the Lord, and stay upon his God." Underscore this phrase: "Trust in the name of the Lord." Look to Him. It sounds so elementary, does it not?

You see, it is not necessary for you to know why. "Ours is not to reason why," wrote the poet, "Ours is to do or die." "Why?" is not your question. It is God's question. *How* is your question. *Why* is why it happened. *How* is your response to it. When we trust during dark times, it is not blind faith. In fact, faith in Christ, even in the darkness, is a *seeing believing*. Faith is not irrational. It is practical and purposeful.

Warren Wiersbe commented, "We don't live by explanation. We live by promises." God is under no obligation to explain Himself to us, even though we sometimes wish He were. Even if He did explain Himself to us, with our finite minds we probably would not be able to grasp His meaning.

> Oh, the depth of the riches both of wisdom and knowledge of God! How unsearchable are His judgments and unfathomable His ways! For who has known the mind of the Lord, or who became His counselor? or who has first given to Him that it might be paid back to Him again? (Rom. 11:33-35, NASB)

The Psalmist sang, "O God, thy ways are past finding out." Jack R. Taylor wrote, "Faith is an act and an affirmation of that act that bids eternal truth to be present fact." And truth is truth in darkness or light. We live not by explanation, but by promises. There it is.

Thomas Watson remarked, "Where reason cannot wade, faith must swim." Just trust God. Turn through your Bible, and the promises of God will leap out at you. Hang onto them. Believe them. Accept them. You do not have to understand it to stand on it. I do not understand electricity, but I have it in the house. I do not understand aerodynamics, but I catch a plane when I have to. In order to live, people have to exercise all kinds of faith. They believe in the bus driver, the airplane pilot, the cook in the restaurant.

When you find yourself in the darkness, and you do not have the slightest notion what to do, trust Him. "Let him trust the name of the Lord." This is the highest pinnacle of faith. Faith does not rise to the top when you can see your way clear. It does when nothing seems to make sense. Job finally came to the place where he relented and affirmed, "Though he slay me, yet will I trust him" (Job 13:15). Do not look to any explanation or to any experience.

Look to the Lord. What is the sign you are looking to the Lord? *You obey*. There it is. "Trust and obey. To be happy in Jesus, but to trust and obey."

Tragically, what most Christians do when they pass through the darkness is to stop serving the Lord. They feel that unless everything is "hunkie dorie," they can do nothing at all for the Lord. Nothing is further from the truth. No, that is not the tack to take. Instead, keep on praying. You may reply, "But in the darkness I don't feel like praying." Pray anyway. Jonah in the belly of the great fish prayed like he had never prayed before. Death was upon him. The gastric juices of the whale's belly were stifling him. It was pitch black. That is why the Bible likens the belly of the whale to the grave, "sheol" in the Old Testament. But Jonah prayed anyhow.

Paul and Silas prayed at midnight in the dreadful jail of Philippi. We are to pray "in the night seasons and all the day long." One old song goes, "Just keep on praying 'til light breaks through."

Pray when you *don't* feel like it. Pray until you *do* feel like it. "Pray without ceasing" (1 Thess. 5:17). The late and great Dr. Huber Drumwright put it well:

> Our Lord called for persistence in prayer both by precept and example. In two significant parables Luke underscored the Lord's commendation of the persevering attitude in prayer. The parable of the friend at midnight (11:5-13) afforded Jesus the opportunity to say that "even though he will not get up and give him *anything* because he is his friend, yet because of his persistence he will" (11:8).[2]

Even when you do not understand, remember:

> Likewise the Spirit also helpeth our infirmities: for we know not what we should pray for as we ought: but the Spirit itself maketh intercession for us with groanings which cannot be uttered (Rom. 8:26).

How can you miss? You see, you are not praying by yourself. The Spirit is praying through you and for you, helping to present your petitions to the Father, petitions that perhaps you yourself are not even capable of expressing. God does not hear your prayers because of your emotions. Do not approach God with your hands full of the brass of your emotions. Rather, approach Him with hands and heart full of the sweet incense of His worth. Just keep praying.

In the darkness, not only keep on praying, but keep on *praising*. Paul and Silas praised at midnight. Jonah praised in the belly of the fish. "Then Jonah prayed to the Lord his God out of the fish's belly . . . Then I said, I am cast out of thy sight; yet I will look again toward thy holy temple. . . . But I will sacrifice unto thee with the voice of thanksgiving; I will pay that that I have vowed. Salvation is of the Lord. And the Lord spake unto the fish, and it vomited out Jonah upon the dry land" (2:1,4,9-10).

Even in the dark despair of the great fish's belly, Jonah began to pray. When, in his praise session, he shouted, "Salvation is of the Lord," what happened? As though that were a cue, the fish became sick at his stomach and vomited Jonah onto dry land. Praise precedes powerful progress. Prayer and praise. If Jonah could pray and praise in that condition, what should we do?

Look to the Lord. Lean on the Lord. "Let him trust in the name of the Lord and stay upon his God." That word *stay* is captivating. It is the root of the word for staff, as in Psalm 23. "Thy rod and thy *staff*, they comfort me." The staff, of course, was the stick or pole the shepherd leaned on to keep him from stumbling and falling. He also used it to guide and prod the sheep. The staff usually had a crook which the shepherd could use to pull the straying sheep back into the fold. Can you imagine the shepherd going through a dark valley, leaning on his staff to balance himself? This term *stay* means that we must lean upon the Lord as the shepherd depended on his staff. "Leaning on the everlasting arms."

One reason God puts you in the darkness is so you will learn how to lean. God is not in the business of giving you all the reasons. What you have with Him is a *relationship*. God is in the process of drawing you closer and closer to Him. Sometimes—and I emphasize sometimes—God will have to take everything away so all you will have left is Him. You are to lean on Him—not a sermon, not a formula, not a procedure, not your health, not your bank account, not your glibness.

Francis Quarles understood the meaning of this relationship.

> If I have lost my path, great Shepherd, say,
> Shall I wander in a doubtful way?
> Lord, shall a lamb of Isr'el's sheepfold
> stray?
>
> Thou art the pilgrim's path; the blind man's eye;
> The dead man's life; on thee my hopes rely;
> If Thou remove, I err; I grope; I die.
>
> Disclose thy sun-beams, close Thy wings and stay;
> See, see, how I am blind, and deaf, and stray,
> O Thou, that art my Light, my Life, my Way.

We may admit that God is necessary, but how many of us honestly know that God is enough? In fact, more than enough. To find out if God is enough for you, let me ask these questions. Where do you obtain your joy? Is it from the Lord or somewhere else? If your joy is from your health, then if it goes, your joy will fly out the window. Many a believer has lost his health, his business, his family, his reputation, but has still maintained his joy because the source of genuine contentment and peace is in God. "Stay upon his God." Indeed one may not know that God is enough until God is all one has.

That happened to Job. He lost his family, his servants, his stock, his houses, his properties, his self-esteem, his reputation, and his friends. Yet, he saw the Lord, even in the worst of circumstances. Job spoke prophetically of none other than the Lord Jesus:

> For I know that my redeemer liveth, and that he shall stand at the latter day upon the earth: And though after my skin worms destroy this body, yet in my flesh I shall see God: Whom I shall see for myself, and mine eyes shall behold; and not another; though my reins be consumed within me (Job 19:25-27).

Through the eyes of faith, Job uttered one of the most remarkable prophesies of Christ in the Bible. Job still hoped in the Lord. Sometimes God leads His dear children to the ash heap as He did Job. There we may learn that God is not only necessary but enough, more than enough. It is not why but *Whom* that matters, not rhyme or reason but a personal relationship, not explanation but a promise.

We also may reach our own personal Brook Jabbok, as did Jacob, when he wrestled with the angel and affirmed, "I will not let thee go until you bless me." Jacob struggled with the angel all night long—in the darkness. If you are never in the darkness alone with Jesus, maybe you do not know Him as well as you think you do. The darkness may come, and the darkness may hide, but it cannot divide. Jesus is there in those shadows. "Standing somewhere in the shadows you'll find Jesus . . . and you'll know Him by the nailprints in His hands." You will come to trust and understand Him not from philosophy, not from an outline, not from an abstract principle, but from communion with Him alone

Yet, perhaps God cannot trust you with a dark hour of the soul. When He does, you will pass through the darkness. When you come out of it, you will definitely realize that the light is far more lovely, because you have learned from the darkness. If there were not darkness, would you appreciate the light? It is understandable why many people crack emotionally in the Arctic regions where it may be daylight for six months of the year and then nighttime for the other six months. One, *look to the Lord*. Two, *lean on Him*. Three, *leave it with the Lord*.

Remember Isaiah 50:11.

> Behold, all ye that kindle a fire, that compass yourselves about with sparks: walk in the light of your fire, and in the sparks that ye have kindled. This shall ye have of mine hand; ye shall lie down in sorrow.

In other words, leave it with the Lord. Do not light your own fire. You could make a mess. You may not only end up catching yourself on fire, but you will lie down in sorrow.

"Let's do something, even if it's wrong!" seems to be the mistaken slogan of many who are in the darkness. "Anything but this!" They light their own fire. They grab the proverbial bull by the horns and end light their own fire. They grab the proverbial bull by the horns and end up being gored! They launch out in the energy of the flesh, not waiting upon God. With calloused and profane hands, they take things into their own hands. They do and act contrary to the leadership of the Holy Spirit, and it boomerangs on them.

You must learn a lesson about the darkness. Darkness is the absence of light. There cannot be darkness unless the light is taken away. You cannot go into a room and "turn on the dark." You can, however, enter a room and turn on the light. You cannot turn on the dark. All you can do is flick a switch and *turn off the light*. The darkness never chases the light away. It is always the other way around.

Darkness descends upon the earth when the day goes. The night does not chase the day away. The day simply retreats as the sun goes down. When the sun comes up in the morning it chases the darkness away. The darkness always flees before the light; the light never flees before the darkness because the light is invincible against the darkness. Therefore, God is light. He is the Light of the world. If you are living for Him—yes, fearing Him and obeying Him according to Isaiah 50:10—and if you are in a dark period, it is because of this fact: God has ordained that there be darkness for you. And it is not because the darkness overcame the light. It is because God in His sovereign plan has withdrawn the light. That is God's plan because He is putting you through *the discipline of darkness*. Nothing went wrong. God has chosen you as one of His special ones. But if you are not careful, you will play with matches and light your own fire.

Manmade light is always deceptive. It reminds me of a person trying to read a sundial at night in order to tell the time, so he pulls out a flashlight and shines it on the sundial. That is ridiculous. The sundial is meant to register the time by heaven's light, the sun. But many people today walk in the sparks from the fire they have kindled. Many supposed Christians are running here and there, tossed to and fro by every wind of doctrine.

The Bible is chock full of people who built their own fires and took things into their own hands. Abraham, the father of the Hebrew nation, was personified by faith. He was called "the friend of God." God revealed Himself to Abraham in the Ur of the Chaldees. Abraham loved God, feared God, and obeyed God. The Lord had made a covenant with Abraham: "And I will make of thee a great nation, and I will bless thee, and make thy name great; and thou shalt be a blessing: And I will bless them that bless thee, and curse him that curseth thee: and in thee shall all families of the earth be blessed" (Gen. 12:2-3). God further promised to give Abraham and Sarah (Sarai) his wife a son in their old age. Abraham was in the light when God gave him that promise. And then God Himself put Abraham out in darkness.

What happened is that God did not seem to be in a hurry about His promise of a great nation since Abraham and Sarah were becoming elderly. They could not understand why God was seemingly doing nothing. The founder of the Hebrew nation was plunged into darkness and despair, and it was because of God's testing. God was proving Abraham, testing him, and God was also working on His timetables. Compute this. With God, *timing* is more important than *time*.

But then Abraham's faith weakened, and he decided to light his own fire and "do his own thing." He could not wait any longer. So, he decided to produce a son by his servant girl Hagar, instead of his wife Sarah. Ishmael was born, and to this day the descendants of Abraham are lying down in sorrow because of his fire. The descendants of Ishmael are, of course, the Arabs who are fighting Israel tooth and toenail. The newspapers and newscasts chronicle the heartbreak and bloodshed as the sons of Ishmael war against the sons of Isaac, who was later born to Abraham and Sarah as the true son of promise. For almost 3,900 years the sons of Abraham have suffered because of their father's impetuous act.

He could not trust God, could not wait on God, could not look to the Lord, could not lean on the Lord, could not leave it to the Lord.

What about Moses the Lawgiver? God commanded him, "Moses, I

want you to deliver My people from the land of bondage, Egypt. You are going to be my commander-in-chief, and I want you to obey Me." Then Moses became jittery and nervous about it. He could not understand what was keeping the Lord. He lit his own fire. In a fit of rage he murdered an Egyptian. Meant to be a missionary, Moses ended up being a murderer. After that headstrong act, he spent forty years on the backside of the desert, every night lying down in sorrow, because he could not trust himself into the hands of God. He had to make things happen, and he goofed.

Simon Peter—"Rocky" they would call him today—was a macho, take-charge guy. He was like a bull in a china shop. He was the first to speak and the first to act—with impetuosity. In Gethsemane he cut off the ear of Malchus, the high priest's servant. Jesus had foretold He was going to suffer, bleed, and die on the Cross, be buried, and rise again the third day. To Peter it looked like the tide had turned. Peter simply could not understand. He could think of nothing else to do, so he reacted with violence. Then, later on he slinked off into the darkness to deny his Lord three times before the sunrise.

When the darkness comes it is *not unusual, not unfruitful, not unending*. From your darkness, *look to the Lord, lean on Him, leave it with Him*. Have faith in God. God is necessary, and He is also enough. "He's everything I need."

Years ago a father and his little girl returned from the cemetery where they had buried his wife, her mother. The house was empty without her. Mother was gone.

The little girl went to her bedroom, the father to his bed, now cold and empty. The girl called from her room, "Daddy, Daddy, can I sleep with you tonight?"

The dad replied, "Of course, darling." So the daughter crawled into the bed. They turned out the light.

"Daddy," the little girl whispered, "it sure is dark. I believe it's the darkest night I've ever seen." He answered, "Yes, dear, I believe it's the darkest night I've ever seen."

Then she said, "Daddy, I can't even see you. Daddy, is your face toward me?" "Yes," her dad answered. "Yes, precious, Daddy's face is toward you."

She asked, "Daddy, you can love through the dark, can't you?"

"Yes, darling, daddy can love you right through the dark. Daddy does love you and, honey, go to sleep." She went to sleep, and that daddy slipped out of bed and fell down on his knees. He prayed to God, "Oh God, God, it's dark. I don't believe I've ever seen it so dark."

And the Father answered, "Yes, Son, it's dark."

"Father, is your face toward me?"

"Yes, my Son, my face is toward you."

"Father, you can love me through the dark, can't you?"

"Yes, my child, I do love you, no matter how dark it is. I love you."

And the man climbed back into bed and fell asleep.

Even in the darkness, God's face is toward you. He loves you through the dark. That darkness can hide, but it cannot divide. Look to the Lord. Lean on the Lord. And leave it with Him.

11. Weeding the Garden

If life hands you a lemon, make lemonade!
—Author Unknown

Otto Von Bismarck was the chancellor of Germany during the First World War. Adolph Hitler was profoundly influenced by him. It is no wonder. Bismarck "carried the bile of bitterness and the inner seethings of resentment. When he had no immediate cause for hate, he would dredge up a skeleton from the past and chew on it for awhile.

"One morning Bismarck proudly announced, 'I have spent the whole night hating.' So, the weight of resentment eventually broke his health. He grew a beard to hide the twitching muscles of his face. Jaundice, gastric ulcers, gallstones, and shingles wracked his body. . . . When a publisher offered him a large sum of money for his life's story, he began to write with a reckless disregard for truth, heaping hate on men and women long dead. Hatred was Bismarck's passion. He died at eighty-three, an embittered, cynical, desperately lonely old man, miserable and self-consumed."[1]

Bitterness is a blight, an emotional cancer which consumes many a person who once had the bloom of eternal springtime upon them. Behind nearly every church squabble, bitterness is lurking somewhere in the shadows. Bitterness reveals itself in a person who is caustic, critical, overloaded with resentment, faultfinding, anger, and animosity. Unfortunately, people like that are in the churches, in our places of work, and maybe in our homes. And all of us should ask ourselves: *Am I bitter? Or, do I have the seeds of its bitter fruit in me?*

The embittered person has trouble facing his bitterness because, most of the time, he truly believes his sour outlook on life is justified. Thus, bitterness is deeply ingrained and not simple to solve.

And bitterness—and I could wear out the negative adjectives—is horrible, hellish, and hurtful.

The Word cautions us:

> Follow peace with all men, and holiness, without which no man shall see the Lord. Looking diligently lest any man fail of the grace of God; *lest any root of bitterness springing up trouble you, and thereby many be defiled* (Heb. 12:14-15, author's italics).

First of all, let us focus on . . .

THE ROOT OF BITTERNESS

What is the root of bitterness, and how does this root begin to grow beneath the surface of our lives? A bitter person is usually one who has been hurt. Perhaps he/she was abused as a child, was often rejected by others, was unsuccessful in friendships and love relationships, was fired from a job, or was even bypassed at church.

During the Christmas season of 1987 bitterness was splattered across the front pages of the papers and on the TV screens because it was first splattered literally against walls, on cars, and on the ground. In my remembrance never was there such a demonic wave of mass murders. In Arkansas a man with a long history of bitterness was accused of killing sixteen of his relatives. Another man allegedly killed eight in Missouri. Several more multiple murders were reported across the nation.

All of these suspected murderers had profiles in common, including an immense backlog of bitterness, fits of depression, inferiority complexes, and dreadful self-images. Somewhere these people were hurt. That hurt smoldered and finally flamed up in murderous anger and hostility.

Is there a person among us that has not been hurt? I have never encountered a man or woman who has not been wounded emotionally and spiritually sometime. It usually began in childhood. We adults could sympathize with children better if we would recall the hurts of our childhood. When we are hurt our natural inclination is first to withdraw into a defensive shell, then to react with anger and resentment, and maybe a desire to get even.

If we are Christians the desire for revenge is absolutely wrong. That is of the old nature before Christ made His residence with us. What do we do? We must confess it, deal with it, and put it behind us. Then it will not become a root of bitterness.

As we continue to deal with the blight of bitterness, consider what it can do. According to Ralph Speas, author of *How to Deal with How You Feel,* bitterness or resentment *damages relationships*. It grows; causes trouble; defiles; *deteriorates the personality; damages spiritual vitality,* and *it destroys*.[2]

When a bitter person is hurt, he does not pause to grapple with his hurt but allows it to fester. He dwells on it, and mulls it over in his mind. In order to justify this nasty emotion, he tries to ferret out the problems of others.

If another person hurts him, even if that person did it unknowingly, the bitter one looks for faults in him/her. The embittered one accentuates the negative. He is seldom capable of being positive. If he sounds positive, such is often contrived or insincere. He builds his mental dossier of others' failings. Of course, he will find them in abundance. Except for Jesus all of us have flaws.

The more faults he finds, the more he feels confirmed in his state of bitter guile. Strangely enough, people capable of deep-seated bitterness are usually intelligent people. Naïve people are often a blessing because they overlook hurts and putdowns, perhaps not even being aware that anyone is intending to slam them.

I must confess. There are caustic Christians and sour saints. I wish that were not the case. At least they make a claim of being Christians, and I cannot look into their hearts. They are also crafty and clever. They seem to have a knack of infecting others with their bitterness. These bitter believers seem to understand which buttons to push in order to receive the response they want. They want to "get under your skin," so they can make you react with hostility toward them. That once again reinforces their bitterness, which is then even more validated in their subconscious.

Anna Russell's poem is priceless:

> I went to see my psychiatrist to be
> psychoanalyzed.
> To find out why I killed my cat and
> blackened my wife's eyes.
> He put me on a downy couch to see
> what he could find,
> And this is what he dredged up from
> my subconscious mind.
> When I was one my mommy hid my dolly
> in the trunk.
> And so it follows naturally that I
> am always drunk.
> When I was two I saw my father kiss the
> maid one day,
> And that's why I suffer now from
> kleptomania.
> When I was three I suffered ambivalence
> from my brothers,
> And so it follows naturally that I
> poisoned all my lovers.
> I'm so glad I have learned the lesson
> it has taught
> That everything I do is someone else's
> fault.[3]

The poem is facetious—at the same time true. The embittered one is not merely angry, depressed, or hurt. He is not willing to wrestle with his hateful, vindictive spirit; rather it is always somebody else's fault. "Look what they did to me. My parents, my associates, the police, the system, my fellow workers, my bosses . . . *they!*"

The root of bitterness expands in the soil of a hurt which was unforgiven and allowed to bury itself deeply in the heart and mind. We have glanced at *the root of bitterness,* and now we address . . .

THE FRUIT OF BITTERNESS

"Looking diligently lest [for fear] any man fail of the grace of God, lest any root of bitterness springing up trouble you, and thereby many be defiled" (Heb. 12:15).

Yes, the bitter person hurts others, but guess who he hurts the most? Himself. It will "trouble you." He is in trouble relationally to God and toward his fellowman. His bitterness is infectious like the AIDS. Soon it becomes contagious and contaminates those who are around him.

There is *personal* trouble from bitterness. Remember Count Von Bismarck. But then there will be *social* trouble resulting from bitterness.

Twenty-five years ago Dr. S. I. McMillen published a book that has now sold millions of copies, *None of These Diseases*.[4] Dr. McMillen, a Christian physician, pointed out what negative feelings could do not only to the emotions but also to the body as well. His book was a Christian examination of psychosomatic medicine.

In that book he lists over fifty diseases that may be caused by destructive, sinful emotions—anger, anxiety, stress, bitterness, hatefulness, and unforgiveness, for instance. Many people are sick physically, but the factors behind the sickness are oftentimes emotional and psychic.

I am not indicating that every sick person is bitter. Sickness is coming to all of us eventually, but every bitter person who does not deal with his emotional-spiritual upset will ultimately be sick. When you become bitter with others, you become a slave to them.

Dr. McMillen wrote, "The man I hate may be many miles from my bedroom, but more cruel than any slavedriver he whips my thoughts into such a frenzy that my innerspring mattress becomes a torture. The lowliest of the serfs can sleep, but not I. I really must acknowledge the fact that I am a slave to every man upon whom I pour the vial of my wrath."[5]

Bitterness can kill you by degrees. You may ask, "But if a person is bitter like that, how can he live eighty-three years or more, like Bismarck?" That is part of their torment, I guess. They are dying, eaten alive by their own bitterness, but not able to die. The bitter person is committing emotional suicide, but sometimes physical decease is slow in arriving.

An ancient Roman story goes: the soldiers of Caesar became dissatisfied with their regimen and rations. They could not complain to Caesar, so they became angry with the gods. So, many of them shot their arrows toward the heavens, hoping to hit the gods. Several of the soldiers were wounded or killed as their own arrows, with high velocity, fell back upon their heads. What an apt illustration of what bitterness does to a person.

There will be *physical* trouble. There will be *emotional* unrest. And there will be *spiritual* trouble.

Verse 14 encourages us to "Follow peace with all men and holiness without which no man shall see the Lord." You cannot have hellishness and holiness in the heart at the same time. And so in the same sentence the text mentions peace with all men and holiness. Then the Word continues with the warning against bitterness.

Yes, bitterness will cause personal trouble, but many may be defiled through it. Like atomic fission which explodes the atomic bomb or warhead, so bitterness has a chain reaction.

"A brooding anger is often linked to resentment [bitterness]. . . . Jesus said we shouldn't be angry without a cause. Wrong anger is anger minus a reason."[6]

Even though bitterness may have started with an actual wrong, the

Christian should seek to understand his bitterness, confess it, repent of it, and forgive the person who has wronged him. Most of us have a general idea of who has hurt or offended us, but consider this true case.

A woman knew for a fact that her son was killed by a Japanese sniper from first-hand reports from her late son's buddies who were with him when he was killed. For years she hated anyone who faintly resembled an Oriental—be they Chinese, Japanese, Korean, Thai, Cambodian, Laotian, Burmese, whoever.

After several years she was talking with her pastor about it and in tears, she blurted out, "I can't hold that grudge any longer. That Japanese boy, like my son, was just doing his job as a soldier. Maybe he was later killed by an American, and it wouldn't be fair for that Japanese mother to hold all white men responsible for killing her son. And besides, Jesus forgave us for crucifying Him and putting Him on the Cross, so I figure the least I can do is to forgive that boy, even though I don't know his name and don't know whether he's alive or dead."

The Bible teaches that there are times when we can be angry and not sin. "Be ye angry and sin not," goes the first part of Ephesians 4:26. Sometimes anger is justifiable. Jesus was righteously angry when He drove the moneychangers from the Temple. But our Lord was never bitter. The second half of Ephesians 4:26 amplifies the situation: "Let not the sun go down upon your wrath." If I understand it, wrath is anger turned bitter, driven into the subconscious mind where it festers and smolders. That is why you ought not to sleep upon your anger. Resolve it before the end of the day and before going to bed. So many marriages could be saved if husbands and wives would kiss and make up before he ends up sleeping on the couch or she packs her bags and goes home to mama, and the "better half" becomes the *bitter* half.

Bitterness is not born overnight. It grows as anger is unresolved and becomes wrath, and wrath contains the seeds of hell. In connection with verse 26 consider 27: "Neither give place to the devil." Giving place to the devil means you allow him to have a toehold in your emotions. Before you are aware he has his feet in the door—and then both legs. Bitterness becomes the devil's campground, his beachhead.

Satan gloats when the Christian becomes angry and then bitter. Then he can make you lose your testimony and virtually, your rationality. That bitterness becomes a "stronghold," and the devil uses it as a launching pad for flights of fancy, "imaginations" and "every high thing that exalteth itself against the knowledge of God" (see 2 Cor. 10:4-5).

What a difference it would make if we would heed the Word of God, instead of what some new age, humanistic practitioner propounds. In Ephesians the apostle was speaking about the kind of relations the brothers and sisters in Christ ought to have. Ephesians 4:31: "Let all bitterness, and wrath, and anger, and clamour, and evil speaking, be put away from you, with all malice."

"Put away" means to dispose of them, deal with them, discard them. We have a fairly good idea of what bitterness is. It is resentment, based on hurts real or imagined, which we have blown out of all proportion. It carries with it a built-in intent for revenge or "getting even."

"The list of sins in verse 31 all have to do with bad temper. 'Bitterness' describes the sour, resentful spirit of a person who broods over the injuries and slights he receives and refuses to be reconciled. 'Wrath' is literally a sudden outburst of passion; 'anger' is a settled feeling. Such eruptions of temper show themselves both in 'clamour' and in 'evil speaking.' The first of these words likely refers to public quarreling; the latter word may be taken in this context to mean slanderous whispers. These things, together 'with all malice,' are to be decisively 'put away.' The Greek word for 'malice' may be defined as 'a vicious disposition.' or 'spite.' Moulé understands it as 'the deep *unkindness*' of the self-centered, Christless heart. Certainly, it should have no place in a believer's life."[7]

Bitterness. Wrath. Anger. Clamor (clamour in the King James). Evil speaking. Malice. All of them are associated with bitterness. Unless these are controlled and put under the blood of Christ, they could burst into flames one of these days. For the unbeliever it could be an afternoon of mass killings. For the believer it might even be physical abuse of another person or maybe a violent burst of outrage. It happens all the time, unfortunately. Then the Christian asks, "What happened to me? How could I do that?"

Clamor is when your anger and bitterness become vocal. You snap at another person, you yell, it becomes a verbal contest. You may even vilify the other person. Then the clamor can pass into evil speaking. It is no longer an argument but is now name-calling. You may even say things you don't mean. Many family members and husbands and wives do. "I can't stand you." "I wish I'd never met you." "I want a divorce." "Get out of the house." "I never want to see you again." Or, even, "I hate you!" You speak untruths and things you don't mean. Sometimes it's too late to take them back. In a fit of clamor and evil speaking, lasting harm can be done.

Then the evil speaking can turn into malice, expressed or unexpressed. In other words, I want to do you harm, hurt you, even injure you. That is why the writer of Hebrews warns against letting "any root of bitterness springing up trouble you, and thereby many be defiled." Physically. Emotionally. Spiritually.

Now, we have examined *the root of bitterness* and *the fruit of bitterness* . . . but now . . .

THE PURSUIT OF BITTERNESS

Hebrews 12:15 starts out: "Looking diligently lest any man fail of the grace of God . . ." A root is underground. You have to go after it, find it, and dig it up if it is undesirable. From that standpoint you need to pursue it for three reasons. First, you must pursue it *to recognize it*. Many people will never recognize bitterness in their own lives. If and when a person recognizes it, when he has made a proper diagnosis, he is on the road to recovery from resentment. But most bitter persons are simply not going to confess, "I am bitter, and I need to do something about it right now." They have become adept at looking at the faults of others. Would you be willing to recognize your bitterness?

What happens when you live an outwardly good life but you have bitterness buried within? The outward trappings represent pruning and touching up on the outside, while deep down inside those roots are going deeper and deeper. The more you prune, the more the roots are being strengthened. The contradiction in your life is going to become more severe until you might experience all kinds of emotional, mental, and spiritual diseases. You could finally end up in an institution. In the meantime, you may have defiled and poisoned countless other people who have marched to your funeral dirge.

Pursue it in order *to recognize it*. Honesty is hard to come by for the embittered person. Then you need to pursue it *to remove it*. Root it out. Nothing else will do that but digging back and forgiving those persons who have wounded you.

You must consciously forgive. It is not enough to think forgiveness. You must *actualize* it. Plan to root out your bitterness. Note that Paul, after the passage on bitterness, admonishes:

> And be ye kind one to another, tenderhearted, forgiving one another, even as God for Christ's sake hath forgiven you (Eph. 4:32).

David Augsburger has noted:

> The man who forgives pays a tremendous price—the price of the evil he forgives!
>
> If the state pardons a criminal, society bears the burden of the criminal's deed.
>
> If I break a priceless heirloom that you treasure and you forgive me, you bear the loss and I go free.
>
> Suppose I ruin your reputation. To forgive me, you must freely accept the consequences of my sin and let me go free!
>
> In forgiveness, you bear your own anger and wrath at the sin of another, voluntarily accepting responsibility for the hurt he has inflicted upon you.[8]

If you really forgive, you will not continue to dredge up the past. Many husbands and wives have clashes like this: "Honey, I forgive you, but I remember how you hurt me back in 1972!" That is not forgiveness. No matter how hard it is, forgive. Jesus is our perfect Model of forgiveness in action. I will never fully understand all the meaning of his prayer on the Cross, "Father, forgive them, for they know not what they do." Of course, God the Father did not forgive them unless they repented, but Jesus was revealing God's willingness to forgive. As He was dying for that very reason—to offer forgiveness for the sins of the whole world—no prayer could have been more meaningful for subsequent generations of lost sinners.

How are you possibly going to follow through on forgiveness and restitution? There it is. Forgive "even as God for Christ's sake hath forgiven you." Forgive freely, fully. You are not to seek revenge. "Vengeance is mine, saith the Lord, I will repay" (Deut. 32:35).

Only the grace of God can cause us to forgive. The tendency of the natural, unregenerate person is to hold grudges and not to forgive. When a Christian "fails of the grace of God," that does not imply he has lost his position of salvation, but that he is reacting and acting out of keeping with the grace which provided his salvation. In other words, these negative characteristics are not consistent with his Christian walk.

You may argue, "But the path the Bible outlines is hard." Yes, and Calvary was hard for Jesus. If you are to pursue bitterness and kill its roots, thus alleviating its putrid fruits, then you must have a taste of the Cross. The first verse of this very chapter asks us to "run with patience the race which is set before us" (12:1). Then verse 2 challenges us to look "unto Jesus the author and finisher of our faith; who for the joy that was set before him endured the cross, despising the shame, and is set down at the right hand of the throne of God." He suffered for the joy of forgiving us and for the joy which awaited Him with the Father, the Holy Spirit, and the heavenly host.

I have heard that "forgiveness is the fragrance on the heel that crushed a violet." You may ask, "When I forgive a person, is that going to deal with those memories?" No, unless you have amnesia, some of your memories will remain.

An unknown sage put it like this, "The hornet of remembering may fly again, but the sting of bitterness has been removed." Oh, you may remember it psychologically, but the sting will be gone because you have put that hurt beneath Calvary's blood. And you will be kind, tenderhearted, and forgiving one another, as Christ for God's sake has forgiven you.

Not only are you to pursue it in order *to recognize it* and *to remove it,* but you are also to pursue it in order *to replace it*. It is no accident that Hebrews 12:14 states, "Follow peace with all men, and holiness, without which no man will see the Lord." It is not enough to expel the bitterness. We must want restitution and reconciliation with our brothers and sisters.

I have heard that Edwin Markham the poet reached the age of retirement and found out that his banker had defrauded him. He was ready to retire but was penniless. He came to the place where he could no longer write poetry. Because of his bitterness the candle of joy had been blown out in his heart. He was obsessed with the evil perpetrated against him by a man he had thought was a friend. One day he was sitting at his desk doodling, drawing circles on his paper, not writing poetry but only thinking of the man who had wronged him. Marcum later testified that the Holy Spirit convicted him with, "Marcum, if you do not deal with this thing, it is going to ruin you. You cannot afford the price you are paying. You must forgive that man." The poet prayed, "Lord, I will, and I do freely forgive."

The root of bitterness was pulled out. The joy began to flow, and so did his mind and pen. He then penned perhaps his most famous poem, "Outwitted."

> He drew a circle that shut me out—
> Heretic, rebel, a thing to flout;

But Love and I had the wit to win:
We drew a circle that took him in!

There is the solution to bitterness. Someone has harmed you and wronged you. Bitterness has been so strong you could almost taste it as bile within your mouth. Pursue that bitterness. With the Spirit's spade root it out. Draw a circle that takes in those who have wronged you. Forgive them for Christ's sake!

From pettiness and that desire
Which goads one to retaliate;
With patience I would quench the fire
Of vengeance, ere it be too late.

And in defeat may I cast out
The moods of envy and despair,
And from my heart, Lord, I would rout
All bitterness. This is my prayer.[9]

NOTES

1. G. Curtis Jones, *1000 Illustrations for Preaching and Teaching* (Nashville: Broadman Press, 1986), p. 219.
2. Ralph Speas, *How to Deal with How You Feel* (Nashville: Broadman Press, 1980), pp. 40-43.
3. This poem is attributed to Anna Russell. Every effort has been made to find the original source.
4. S. I. McMillen, *None of These Diseases* (Old Tappan, New Jersey: Fleming H. Revell, 1963).
5. Ibid., p. 35.
6. Speas, Ibid., p. 70.
7. W. Curtis Vaughn, *The Letter to the Ephesians* (Nashville: Convention Press, 1963), pp. 103-104.
8. David W. Augsburger, *Seventy Times Seven: The Freedom of Forgiveness* (Chicago: Moody Press, 1970), p. 20.

9. Margaret E. Bruner, quoted in *Masterpieces of Religious Verse*, ed. by James Dalton Morrison (Nashville: Broadman Press, paperback edition, 1977, originally published by Harper & Row, 1948), p. 436.

PAUL & CAROLYN WALKER
P. O. Box 61
5804 Northland Dr.
Millington, TN 38053